QUESTIONS ON THE WAY

A catechism based on The Book of Common Prayer

Beverley D. Tucker
William H. Swatos, Jr.

Forward Movement Publications
Cincinnati, Ohio

This is a complete revision of Beverley D. Tucker's previous editions of *Questions on the Way.*

Contents

**To all those,
past, present and future,
from whose questions
this book has taken shape**

✝

And when in time to come your son asks you, "What does this mean?" you shall say to him, "By strength of hand the Lord brought us out of Egypt, from the house of bondage."

Exodus 13:14

When your children ask their fathers in time to come, "What do these stones mean?" then you shall let your children know, "Israel passed over this Jordan on dry ground."

Joshua 4:21-22

Stand by the roads, and look, and ask for the ancient paths, where the good way is; and walk in it, and find rest for your souls.

Jeremiah 6:16

Set up waymarks for yourself, make yourself guideposts; consider well the highway, the road by which you went.

Jeremiah 31:21

They shall ask the way to Zion, with faces turned toward it, saying, "Come, let us join ourselves to the Lord in an everlasting covenant which will never be forgotten."

Jeremiah 50:5

They found him in the temple, sitting among the teachers, listening to them and asking them questions.   *Luke 2:46*

Ask, and it will be given you; seek and you will find; knock, and it will be opened to you.   *Matthew 7:7*

And as he was setting out on his journey, a man ran up and knelt before him, and asked him, "Good teacher, what must I do to inherit eternal life?"   *Mark 10:17*

Seek first his kingdom and his righteousness and all these things shall be yours as well.   *Matthew 6:33*

And he asked them, "But who do you say that I am?" Peter answered him, "You are the Christ."   *Mark 8:29*

They said to each other, "Did not our hearts burn within us while he talked to us on the way, while he opened to us the scriptures?"   *Luke 24:32*

Now when they heard this they were cut to the heart, and said to Peter and the rest of the apostles, "Brethren, what shall we do?"   *Acts 2:37*

Earnestly desire the higher gifts. And I will show you a still more excellent way.   *I Corinthians 12:31*

Thomas said to him, "Lord, we do not know where you are going; how can we know the way?" Jesus said to him, "I am the way, and the truth, and the life."   *John 14:5-6*

Introduction

I came upon Beverley Tucker's *Questions on the Way: a Catechism for Episcopalians* as a seminarian serving a small mission congregation. I needed something I could use with only a few people—or even give to a single individual—who wanted to know more about the Christian faith as the Episcopal Church has received it. There were, I knew, excellent curricula available, but these usually presumed classes of a dozen or more, who could then "divide into small groups." (Indeed, to this day, this instruction remains a standing joke in my congregation.) There were, I also knew, excellent books on various aspects of the Christian life. "The Church's Teaching Series" is among them, but to present a person who says "I want to know more about the Episcopal Church" with a half-dozen volumes constitutes ecclesiastical overkill. This one little book, privately printed, stood out: *Questions on the Way.*

I have used it with teenagers and with people old enough to be the parents of teenagers, with men and women, with people who wish to know something more of what is often a strange and little understood church in their midst. Not all by any means have become Episcopalians, but never has the book been unappreciated. It responds simply and directly to the basic questions people have as they consider their religious lives.

Over the course of time, however, two things happened: *Questions on the Way* went out-of-print, and the Episcopal Church engaged in a monumental revision of its Book of Common Prayer. Initially I solved this problem by lending the catechisms, while giving away copies of the 1928 Book of Common Prayer at the same time so that people could follow the many references. But people did not want to give back Tucker's book, and at length I was down to my last two copies.

I wrote the author and we planned to revise *Questions* to bring it into harmony with the 1979 Book of Common Prayer, the 1982 Hymnal and canonical changes. What Beverley Tucker and I produced is not a revision but a wholly rewritten *Questions on the Way,* edited by Forward Movement Publications' director, Charles H. Long, and consulting editor, Robert Horine.

It might be asked why another catechism is necessary since the prayer book already has one which has both a long history and a solid contemporaneity. It is certainly not the purpose of this book to replace the prayer book catechism, 'An Outline of the Faith'; on the contrary, we draw from it and urge all members of the church to know it well. Our intention is to expand upon its content and to concentrate into one place much of the essential information upon which the prayer book catechism is founded.

Although the primary purpose of this catechism is as an introduction to the Episcopal Church for those outside of it, we hope it will be useful for discussion groups in the congregations, Episcopalian or otherwise.

In a small book such as this, many questions are treated very briefly. Obviously it is impossible to express adequately such mysteries as the Holy Trinity and the Atonement in so short a space. We strongly urge readers to pursue the references we have given to the prayer book and the Bible, and to consult with a member of the clergy for additional books and sources. We also wish that the reader would approach the catechism prayerfully, asking God's gifts for understanding, humility, devotion and zeal.

We do not have all the answers. Indeed, the first thing we can tell you is that anyone who claims to tell you "all the answers" in things pertaining to God doesn't have them—and may not have any. But as fellow pilgrims on the way to a heavenly city we will share with you what we have of the one who leads us: Jesus Christ, the same yesterday, today, and forever.

William H. Swatos, Jr.

Silvis, Illinois
The Epiphany, 1987

I Religion

1. **Q.** What is a catechism?
   A. A catechism is a summary of religious teaching, often in question and answer form. Christian catechisms teach us the essentials of the Christian life. In the Book of Common Prayer (abbreviated as BCP hereafter) there is "An Outline of the Faith, commonly called the Catechism" (pp. 845-862). This book is intended to supplement that.

2. **Q.** Do we need faith to live by?
   A. Yes. Life requires us to make decisions, and faith enables us to decide. We all believe something, and we all depend on implicit assumptions—our senses, our reason, the tools we use, science, the state, a world spirit, God. When we make these implicit assumptions explicit to our consciousness and act upon them we have "faith." Religion is faith with its influence on our thoughts and actions.

3. **Q.** Granted that there are many faiths, does it matter *what* we believe?
   A. Yes, because what we believe determines who we are, what we do, and the purpose for which we live.

4. **Q.** Is it not true that science can explain everything, and if so, do we need any faith except science?
   A. Science can explain many things, but there are other things which are of the highest importance which are outside the realm of science. Science cannot make values, nor decide on priorities, nor tell what is morally right or wrong. Science cannot explain beauty, love, good and evil, the freedom of our wills, art, music, the purpose for which we live, what happens after death, or why and how the universe could be created out of nothing. Science knows nothing of God or of the human spirit. In short, most of

7

the things which give our lives meaning and uniqueness are outside the realm of science.

5. **Q.** Are science and faith contradictory?
A. No. Science and faith deal with reality and truth on different levels and ask and answer different questions. Both are important and necessary, and each complements the other.

6. **Q.** With what does science deal?
A. Science seeks to explain a part of reality on one level and to attain truth in the physical world through the use of our perceptions and reason. The physical sciences deal with the created universe. The social sciences deal with people and society, and they often share the same concerns as religion, but science cannot, of itself, assign values and priorities nor determine goals.

7. **Q.** With what does religion deal?
A. Religion seeks to find the meaning of this world and our place and purpose in it. Religion deals with ethics and values, with our relationships to each other and to the world, and with what happens after death. Religion seeks to know God and the relationship between God and ourselves. Religion tries to find out God's will for us.

8. **Q.** How can we know God?
A. The Christian faith teaches us that we can come to know God through God's revelation in creation, through the testimony of seekers of God in all ages, through the special revelation in the Bible, and supremely in Jesus Christ. Although we human beings with our finite minds cannot "prove" God or the "existence" of God, belief in God enables us to understand many things which otherwise would be inexplicable, such as the origin and purpose of the universe. Without belief in God, we are mere chemical accidents, puppets in a mechanistic universe,

without freedom, meaning, or purpose, and our end is meaningless death in the face of blind forces leading to ultimate chaos. But Christian faith is a living, personal relationship of love for, trust in, and active commitment to the God who loves us, who created and sustains us, and who gives us the purpose of our being.

9. **Q.** How do we know that Christianity is the true religion? **A.** There is no objective, scientific way to prove it, and we can only verify it by deciding for it and living it. However, there are a number of things about Christianity which ought to make us consider it seriously. Christianity is the largest religion in the world and most international, with about 1,000,000,000 believers. It is the faith which has been held by many of the world's great scholars and scientists, and it has been the inspiration and heart of some of the world's great cultures and works of art. Even though it has been attacked and persecuted repeatedly for almost 2,000 years, the Christian faith has been kept fast by men and women who were ready to die for it in all nations, and it is still growing today.

10. **Q.** If Christianity is the true religion, why are Christians imperfect, and why are there wars in and between Christian nations? **A.** There has never been any completely "Christian" person except Jesus Christ. To say that Christians are not perfect is merely to say that they are not completely Christian, which they would freely admit. Likewise, there are no really Christian countries or societies, for none of them perfectly follows the way of Christ. Wars and other social evils are the result of this failure.

11. **Q.** If Christianity is the true religion, why are there so many denominations? **A.** Although truth is one, we see it from different angles. As we draw nearer to truth, our beliefs, like spokes in a

wheel, will grow closer together. Even though there are many denominations in Christianity which are the result of our imperfections, inadequate understanding, and the conflicts of history and society, still our faith is the same in the important fundamentals.

12. **Q.** What ways do we have for coming to know God?
A. We can know something of God through our reason and through seeing God's creation, including ourselves as a part of that creation. Through our consciences, and through the testimony of others, particularly in the church, we can learn more. But most of all, we can come to know God through the Bible. Christians believe that the Bible gives us a unique and full revelation of God such as can be found in no other place (Acts 14:17; 17:23-28; Rom. 1:20; Heb. 1:1-2.)

Questions to Think About—I

a. If there were no God, how could the universe be created?
b. If we had no religious beliefs, could we distinguish between good and evil?
c. In what ways do science and religion complement each other?
d. If there were no life after death, what reasons would there be for not being completely selfish?

II The Bible

13. **Q.** What is the Bible?

    A. The Bible is the proclamation of what God has done for us and God's purpose for our fulfillment. It is made up of many "books" by different people, most of whom lived in the region of Israel between about 2000 BC and 100 AD.

14. **Q.** What are the books of the Bible?

    A. The books of the Bible are in three collections. The Old Testament was written in Hebrew (with a few brief passages in Aramaic) between about 1000 BC and 100 BC. The Apocrypha was written by Jews in the Greek language in the period roughly between 200 BC and 50 AD. The New Testament was written in Greek between about 40 AD and 100 AD. In most English Bibles the books are arranged in the following order, according to various classifications, although the Apocrypha is omitted from many Bibles:

The Old Testament

Law—Genesis, Exodus, Leviticus, Numbers, Deuteronomy;

History—Joshua, Judges, Ruth, 1 and 2 Samuel, 1 and 2 Kings, 1 and 2 Chronicles, Ezra, Nehemiah, Esther;

Poetry—Job, Psalms, Proverbs, Ecclesiastes, Song of Solomon;

Prophecy—Isaiah, Jeremiah, Lamentations, Ezekiel, Daniel, Hosea, Joel, Amos, Obadiah, Jonah, Micah, Nahum, Habakkuk, Zephaniah, Haggai, Zechariah, Malachi.

The Apocrypha

1 and 2 Esdras, Tobit, Judith, Additions to Esther, The Wisdom of Solomon, Ecclesiasticus, Baruch, The Letter of Jeremiah, The Prayer of Azariah and the Song of the Three Young Men, Susanna, Bel and the Dragon, The Prayer of Manasseh, 1 and 2 Maccabees.

The New Testament

Gospels—Matthew, Mark, Luke, John;
History—Acts;
Letters—Romans, 1 and 2 Corinthians, Galatians, Ephesians, Philippians, Colossians, 1 and 2 Thessalonians, 1 and 2 Timothy, Titus, Philemon, Hebrews, James, 1 and 2 Peter, 1, 2 and 3 John, Jude;
Apocalyptic—Revelation.

15. **Q.** What does the Old Testament teach us?
A. The Old Testament tells us of the dealings of God with people before the time of Christ, particularly with the people of Israel.

16. **Q.** How was God's nature and God's will shown to people in the Old Testament period?
A. God's nature and will were revealed through history and through particular persons, especially among the people of Israel, like Moses and the prophets, who perceived God's mighty acts in history and interpreted them for us. The manifestation of God's nature and God's will is called *revelation*.

17. **Q.** Who were the people of Israel?
A. The people of Israel were a group of West Asians who looked back to Abraham, Isaac, and Jacob as their ancestors. They were divided into twelve tribes, each of which claimed descent from one of the twelve sons of Jacob, or Israel, as he was also called. God called and

chose Israel to be the recipients of many special revelations (Gen. 12 ff.; Deut. 7:6; Heb. 11:8-19).

18. **Q.** How did God save the people of Israel?
A. When they had become slaves in Egypt, after the time of Joseph (Gen. 37-50), God brought Israel out of Egypt under the leadership of Moses and Aaron about 1280 BC. This is called the *Exodus*. The commemoration of this event became the feast of the *Passover* (Ex. 12-15).

19. **Q.** What did God give to Israel through Moses at Mount Sinai?
A. God made a *covenant* with Israel and gave them the Ten Commandments (Ex. 20). By this covenant God promised to be their God and to bless them, if they would be faithful and follow the commandments, as they pledged to do, so that they might be a blessing to all the peoples on the earth. It is this covenant that gives the Old Testament (or Old Covenant) its name (BCP, p. 846).

20. **Q.** Who led the people of Israel into the promised land of Canaan?
A. Joshua led the twelve tribes of Israel across the Jordan River about 1240 BC, and most of them settled to the west of the river. The charismatic leaders who followed him, like Deborah, Gideon, Jephthah, and Samson, until the time of Samuel, were called the judges (Joshua, Judges, Ruth).

21. **Q.** Who was the first, and who was the greatest king of Israel?
A. Saul was the first king of Israel, and David was the greatest. David unified the twelve tribes of Israel into one nation and established the capital in Jerusalem about 1000 BC (1 & 2 Samuel). In later times after the fall of the kingdom, there was a prophecy that the Savior of the world would appear among the descendants of David (Isa. 11:1; Jer. 23:5).

22. **Q.** What is prophecy?

A. Prophecy is the revelation of God's will. In the Old Testament period there are many prophets, such as Elijah (1 Kings), Elisha (2 Kings), Isaiah, Jeremiah, and Ezekiel. The prophets did not primarily predict the future, but rather they interpreted the history of their times in the light of God's justice. By revealing God's will to their contemporaries, they often help us to see what is God's will for us today.

23. **Q.** When was the temple in Jerusalem built?

A. The first temple in Jerusalem was built during the reign of David's son, Solomon, about 950 BC. It took the place of the tabernacle (tent of meeting) and became the chief place of worship and the only place of sacrifice (1 Kings 5-8). This first temple was destroyed by the Babylonians in 587 BC (2 Kings 25). It was rebuilt on a smaller scale in 520-515 BC, when some of the Jews returned from the Babylonian exile (Ezra 3-6, Haggai, Zechariah). This too was destroyed, and the last temple was built under Herod the Great (37-4 BC). This lasted until the Romans destroyed Jerusalem *c.* 70 AD. The rites and sacrifices of the temple are set forth in Leviticus and other books of the Law.

24. **Q.** Did the kingdom of Israel remain unified from the time of David?

A. No. After Solomon's reign, Israel was divided into two kingdoms: one called Judah in the south; and the other called Israel in the north (1 Kings 12). The northern kingdom was defeated by Assyria in 721, and a large number of the inhabitants were exiled (2 Kings 17). Those who remained in the district of Samaria mingled with other cultures and maintained a mixed religion. The southern kingdom, Judah, with its capital in Jerusalem, was destroyed by the Babylonians under Nebuchadnezzar in 587, and most of the survivors were exiled to Babylon (2 Kings 24-25, Jeremiah). This is known as the *Exile.*

25. **Q.** If the people of Israel were God's chosen people, why were they defeated by other nations, and why did they lose their independence?

A. According to the prophets, Israel was defeated because it rebelled against the will of God and was unfaithful to the covenant by not obeying the Law. The rulers and the wealthy oppressed the poor and corrupted justice. God's choosing of Israel carried a great responsibility as well as a privilege.

26. **Q.** Did Israel (or the Jews, as they were called from that time because of their origin in Judah) return from the Babylonian exile?

A. Some of the Jews did return from their exile in Babylon. Cyrus the Great of Persia conquered Babylon in 539 BC, and during the next century expeditions of Jews were allowed to return to Jerusalem, where they rebuilt the temple between 520 and 516. The priest and scribe, Ezra, helped make the Jews the people of the Law, a religious community or "church" existing in many countries, rather than a nation or a racial group. Synagogues (meaning places to gather together) were built in many countries for worship and study of scripture. The nation might disappear, and Jerusalem and the temple might be destroyed, but the One God still ruled the world. The Jews learned that they could worship God wherever they might be.

27. **Q.** What are the Psalms?

A. The Psalms are a collection of poems or hymns going back to the time of David and later Israelites. Psalms have been used by Jews and Christians as songs of praise, penitence, and thanksgiving for almost 3000 years.

28. **Q.** What is the Wisdom literature?

A. Wisdom literature is a type of writing used in late Judaism, found particularly in Proverbs, Job, Ecclesiastes, and some of the Psalms, which tries to understand God's will for human life, not through revelation in Israel or in history, but through wisdom revealed by God to the human mind.

29. **Q.** What is Apocalyptic writing?
   A. Apocalyptic is a form of allegorical writing which uses fantastic symbols and visions to interpret God's victory and vindication of history and the end of the world. It was written during the times of persecution when the authors wished to conceal the true meaning from their oppressors, and this explains the difficulty of understanding it clearly. Daniel 7-12 is the best example in the Old Testament, and the Revelation to John in the New Testament.

30. **Q.** What was the situation of the Jews in the centuries immediately before and during the New Testament period?
   A. In 332 BC Alexander the Great occupied Palestine and went on to conquer the Persian Empire. This began a long period of Greek or Hellenic influence under his successors, the Ptolemies of Egypt until 198, and the Seleucids of Antioch until 167. Under Judas Maccabeus the Jews rebelled in 168, and in the following year regained their independence (1 Mac. 2-4). This is celebrated in Judaism as the feast of *Hanukkah*. In 63 BC Rome conquered Palestine and ruled it for the next four centuries. In 70 AD a rebellion of the Jews was crushed, and Jerusalem and the temple were utterly destroyed. By this time, however, the majority of Jews lived outside of Palestine, all over the Roman Empire and beyond. These Jews of the dispersion were called the *diaspora*. They built synagogues to worship God and study their religion. Though they spoke the language of the countries where they lived, they remained faithful to the Law of Moses, and their strict moral lives often contrasted strongly with the corrupt society in which they lived.

31. **Q.** What is the Septuagint?
A. The Septuagint was a Greek translation of the Old Testament made in Alexandria, Egypt, about 200 BC. It was supposedly translated by seventy scholars, in seventy days which gives it its name, and this is often referred to by the Roman numerals LXX. A large number of Jews living outside Palestine knew their scriptures mainly through this text, and many outside Judaism also read it and were influenced by it. It is often quoted in the New Testament.

32. **Q.** What is the Apocrypha?
A. It consists of history, poems, proverbs, moral teaching, and stories from the Jewish past, written by Jewish writers in the Greek language (see Q. 14). In the Septuagint these writings were included with the Old Testament, and when this was translated into Latin, they became a part of the Bible of the medieval Church.

33. **Q.** Of what value is the Apocrypha, and how should we use it?
A. Roman Catholics and some other Christians use the Apocrypha as part of the Bible, while many Protestants do not. The Episcopal Church teaches that it can be used for instruction but does not base any doctrines or teachings of the Church on it alone (BCP, p. 853, and p. 868, Article VI). The Apocrypha is a help to bridge the gap between the Old and the New Testaments and to understand better the situation and climate of thought into which Jesus was born.

34. **Q.** Who were the Pharisees?
A. The Pharisees were a party of the Jews from about the time of the Maccabees (168 BC), who emphasized ritual purity and strict observance of the Jewish Law. They built synagogues to spread their teaching and encourage worship and study of the scriptures, and they developed an

17

oral tradition which they valued equally with the written Law of the Bible. They would not associate with Greeks and Romans and other Gentiles, and considered themselves unclean if they had any contact with "sinners," those who did not keep all the Jewish ceremonial laws. They particularly emphasized keeping the Sabbath.

35. **Q.** Who were the Sadducees?

A. The Sadducees were a party of the Jews connected with the ruling priestly families and aristocracy. They controlled the temple, and although they originally had close ties with the Maccabees, many of them became pro-Greek and pro-Roman in an effort to gain favor with the Roman government. Some were corrupt and self-seeking, trying to get more money from the offerings of the people, and they were usually conservative, hoping to maintain themselves in power. They opposed new ideas and, unlike the Pharisees, they rejected the oral traditions and belief in the resurrection and in angels, which were later developments in Judaism.

36. **Q.** What is meant by the term "Messiah," and what ideas do we find about the Messiah in the Old Testament?

A. The word "Messiah" is Hebrew for "anointed" and was used mainly of kings, who were anointed with oil, although priests and prophets were also anointed. After the kingdom of Israel had become weak and divided, a hope grew up that a new king, a descendant of David, would restore glory to Israel and be the savior of the people (Isa. 9:6-7, Jer. 23:5). With this concept of a victorious earthly king were associated other ideas. There was a promise of another prophet, like Moses (Deut. 18:15-18), and of "a priest forever after the order of Melchizedek" (Psalm 110:4; see Gen. 14:18-20). He would be a just judge (Isa. 11:4), and would be called the "Prince of Peace" (Isa. 9:6) and Immanuel (Isa. 7:14). Even David named him "Lord" (Psalm 110:1), and he was to be the Son of God

(Psalm 2:7; 89:26-27). But another prophecy, too profound for most to comprehend, was that one who should be a servant of God would suffer for others and bear their punishment and their griefs, that by his suffering they might be healed (Isa. 53). Finally, in the apocalyptic literature, the Messiah was thought of as a supernatural being, described in mysterious imagery, "one like a son of man," who would come from heaven at the end of the world and bring history to a close (Dan. 7:13-14). In New Testament times all these hopes and ideas contributed to the longing and expectation for God's representative, the anointed one, who should save the people.

37. **Q.** What does the word "Christ" mean?
A. *Christ,* or "Christos," is the Greek word for "Messiah," the anointed one.

38. **Q.** What does the New Testament teach us?
A. The New Testament teaches us of the birth and life of Jesus Christ the Messiah, his teachings and his mighty acts, his death on the cross and resurrection, the coming of the Holy Spirit, and the acts and teachings of the apostles. It is called the New Testament, which means "New Covenant," because of the covenant of salvation which God gave to us through Jesus Christ (1 Cor. 11:25; BCP, p. 850). The New Testament records the clearest and most perfect revelation given us of God's nature, love, and purpose for all people.

39. **Q.** What is the relation between the Old and the New Testaments?
A. The New Testament shows the fulfillment of all that was hoped for and promised in the Old Testament.

40. **Q.** What does the Bible teach us about God?
A. Although the Bible tells us primarily of what God has done for us, and does not give us abstract propositions

about God, we can infer many things from the witness of the Bible. The Bible testifies that there is only One God, who is the Creator of all things. Although God is transcendent and infinite, almighty, eternal, holy, perfect and just, we can know God as a personal Being, who is perfect love. The Bible teaches that God loves us individually, that we can trust God, that we can pray to God, and that God will hear and answer us. God rules over and upholds the whole world and all being, and is its source, bearer and end. God cares for each one of us, for all we do and think, and has a purpose for each of us. In the Old Testament we see God primarily acting in history to redeem Israel. In the New Testament we see the fulfillment of this for all people in the revelation that we can know God most perfectly in Jesus Christ, through whom also we receive redemption (Gen. 1; Deut. 6:4; 32:4; Psalm 90:2; 139:1-14; Isa. 6:3; 46:4; Jer. 32:17-19; 2 Tim. 2:13; 1 John 4:16).

41. **Q.** Why is God called "a jealous God" (Ex. 20:5), and what is meant by "the wrath of God" (Rom. 1:18)?
A. These are metaphorical terms, attempts to express a truth about God in human language. The term, "a jealous God" is used because there is only One God, and any attempt to worship another is a rebellion and a dishonor. "The wrath of God" is an expression which indicates that God, who is love, goodness, and justice, cannot allow hatred, evil, or injustice ultimately to triumph. These metaphorical terms should never be misunderstood to obscure or pose a conflict with God's love and mercy.

42. **Q.** What does the Bible teach us about human beings?
A. The Bible teaches that we are made in the image of God—that is, unlike the animals, we can think and reason, and we have conscience and free will (Gen. 1:27). Though conditioned by heredity and environment, we can transcend them to control ourselves and our lives and influence our environment. We can know God and love

God, just as children love their parents, and through love we can participate in the divine nature. Since "God is love" our love is a reflection or image of God's love (1 John 4:7). We were made to have fellowship with God and cannot truly be ourselves apart from God. But through our self-centeredness and sin we have separated ourselves from God (Luke 15:11-32), and through our failure to love and obey God we have fallen slaves of sin and subjects of death. This truth of our condition is profoundly taught in the parable of Adam and Eve (Gen. 2-3). However, we can see our "original" and intended condition in Jesus Christ.

43. **Q.** What is sin?
A. Sin, in the Christian sense, is rebellion against God, missing the mark, and pride in trying to put ourselves in the place of God. Sin is self-centeredness, instead of God-centeredness. It is selfishness, instead of love. As a result of our sin, we are separated from God, and our relation with others and with our true selves is broken. Sin tries to justify itself and put the blame elsewhere, refusing to take self-responsibility (Gen. 3:12-13). Right from birth we are self-centered. Newborn babies "think" only of themselves. We do not blame them, but it is this same tendency in all people which, later in life, causes our other sins, jealousies, quarrels, and even wars. Because this tendency is in all of us from birth, we call it "original sin." But since we also have reason and conscience to show us the right, and free will to choose the good, we are responsible for our actions, and we are guilty when we sin and choose the evil (Isa. 53:6; Rom. 3:10; 7:19).

44. **Q.** Was God content to see us thus separated by sin from God and each other?
A. No. God continually called us back throughout the history of Israel, through Moses and the prophets, and through the events of history itself. Finally, in the fullness

of time, God intervened in the person of Jesus Christ to bring us back to our "original" fellowship, and into a relationship of reconciliation and love with each other (See the gospels, especially Jn. 1:10-14; 3:16; also 2 Cor. 5:19; 1 Tim. 1:15.)

45. **Q.** How did Jesus Christ accomplish this?
A. In Jesus of Nazareth, God assumed our full humanity and lived a life of perfect love and obedience, even to death on the cross. Through his perfect life and sacrifice on the cross Jesus overcame sin, and in his death and resurrection he conquered eternal death. By identifying ourselves with Jesus through faith, we can participate in his suffering and death, and receive the fruit of his victorious life and resurrection, the forgiveness of our sins, so that we can enjoy new life in the love of God (Rom. 6:3-12; Phil. 2:5-9; Lk. 23:24).

46. **Q.** Was Jesus a human being in the full sense of the word?
A. Yes. The New Testament and the creeds emphasize that Jesus of Nazareth was truly a man, not a "superman," nor God pretending to be human. The gospels record that he was tempted as we are, and that he knew sorrow as well as joy. He wept for his friends, was moved to anger by the money changers in the temple, and showed the common feelings of hunger, thirst, and weariness. He did not *want* to die, and he prayed to God to take away the cup of his suffering (Mk. 14:36). Although God's power was shown through Jesus' miracles, he used it to show mercy, not to impel belief. All during his life Jesus chose the way of humility and love, and showed us what it means to be truly human. Precisely in that he showed us humanity at its highest, he revealed to us the nature of God, and in giving himself for others in love, he expressed the character of God as love. In the man Jesus, we encounter God acting in the world.

47. **Q.** What can we learn from the example of Jesus' life?
A. Jesus gave dignity to manual labor by being a carpenter and by choosing fishermen to be his first disciples. He taught us the value of the individual and of human life by his concern for the sick and the dying, for the weak, the old, the poor, the little ones, the fallen, the despised, and the rejected. He blessed little children and used the gifts of a young boy to feed a multitude. He himself, the Son of Man, was born in a stable, in his public life had nowhere to lay his head, and died betrayed by those he loved, the death of a common criminal. We cannot read the gospels enough, for not only do we find in Jesus the hope of our salvation, but also the pattern of love and obedience for our lives in his perfect life of love. Jesus is our friend and our leader who shows us the way to God and is our companion on the way.

48. **Q.** What is the Atonement?
A. The Atonement means that in Jesus Christ Godhead and humanity were united. We were separated from God by our self-centeredness, our sin, but this separation is overcome by Jesus Christ in his perfect life, sacrificial death on the cross, and victorious resurrection. That is why we call it the "at-one-ment" (Jn. 17:20-23; 2 Cor. 5:17-21).

49. **Q.** What is the New Covenant?
A. The New Covenant is the new relationship with God made possible through the atonement of Christ, promised to us at the Last Supper, sealed with the blood of the cross, and renewed in the offering of the Holy Eucharist (Mk. 14:23-24).

50. **Q.** Did Christ die for us because we had already repented and become good?
A. No. As St. Paul wrote, "God shows his love for us in that while we were yet sinners Christ died for us" (Rom. 5:8). No matter how sinful and separated from God we

may feel, we can be sure that Jesus knows our actual condition and that he loves us and offers us forgiveness.

51. **Q.** Why is Christ called "The Lamb of God, who takes away the sin of the world"?
A. This imagery reflects the Old Testament background and temple practices in the time of Christ. At the feast of the Passover, lambs were sacrificed in commemoration of the redemption of Israel and for the sins of the people, to obtain forgiveness and reconciliation with God (Ex. 12; see also Q. 18). When Christ offered himself on the cross, he made the one perfect and sufficient sacrifice for the sins of the whole world and therefore is called, "the Lamb of God" (see Jn. 1:36; Heb. 5-10).

52. **Q.** Is it correct to say that Jesus was crucified by the Jews?
A. No. Although Jesus was condemned to death by the leaders of the Jews, the Roman government, in other words gentiles, shared full responsibility. Pontius Pilate allowed Jesus to be executed, and it was Roman soldiers who carried out the crucifixion. All people, even the disciples who fled, bear the responsibility. Although the crucifixion was an historical event of the past, its significance is eternal, and if we are to receive the benefits from it, we must acknowledge our share in the guilt, because Jesus died for the sins of all—past, present, and future (Hymn 158; Mt. 25:45; Acts 9:4-5).

53. **Q.** Was Christ's work of salvation finished on the cross?
A. No. Christ's death was not the end of his work of salvation. On the third day God raised him from the dead, and he appeared to his disciples (Mt. 28; Lk. 24; Jn. 20-21; 1 Cor. 15).

54. **Q.** What may we receive through the death and resurrection of Jesus Christ?
A. Through faith in the crucified and risen Christ we

receive forgiveness of our sins, the gift of eternal life, and communion with God. Jesus overcame our two great enemies, sin and death, and is called the pioneer of our salvation (1 Cor. 15:54-57; Heb. 2:10).

55. **Q.** How can we believe in the resurrection and in Christ's miracles?

A. God is the almighty creator of the world and can do all things which are not contrary to the divine character. Therefore, although we believe God usually works through the laws which order the universe, there is no reason to think that God cannot work in ways beyond our understanding. The greatest miracle is that God almighty became a human being like us and died for us, even though we were so unworthy. If, by God's grace, we can believe that, and if we come to know Jesus by faith, the resurrection seems almost inevitable, and Christ's miracles are simply God's power being shown in him. If there had been no resurrection there would be no Church and no Christianity, because the disciples would have scattered in despair, as they were about to do before Jesus appeared to them. It was the resurrection which gave them the faith, joy, and courage to go out to preach the good news to all the world, even in the face of ridicule, persecution, and death. Every week they commemorated the resurrection on Sunday. This became the Christian holy day, The Lord's Day, the *first* day of the week.

56. **Q.** What did the risen Christ do after the resurrection?

A. Christ appeared to the disciples and commanded them to preach the Gospel to all nations, and he promised to be with them always and to give them the power of the Holy Spirit (Mt. 28:19-20; Acts 1:8). On the fortieth day after the resurrection, Christ ascended to reign in Glory (Lk. 28:51; Acts 1:1-11).

57. **Q.** After Christ's ascension how can we be with God in Christ?

A. We can be with God, with the risen and ascended Christ, through the power of the Holy Spirit, whom Christ promised to send (Jn. 15:26).

58. **Q.** When did the Holy Spirit come to the disciples?
A. The Holy Spirit came to the disciples on the day of *Pentecost* (Whitsunday), about fifty days after the resurrection (Easter). The disciples were given a new power, a sense of divine guidance, and a deeper fellowship from the Holy Spirit through whom they experienced Christ in their midst. When Jesus lived on earth, in the days of his flesh, only those in his physical presence could know him. Since Pentecost everyone in every place can know him and experience the presence of God through the indwelling of the Holy Spirit (Acts 2).

59. **Q.** Is the Holy Spirit God?
A. Yes. The Holy Spirit is God, just as the Father and the Son are (Mt. 28:19; 2 Cor. 13:14; Eph. 2:18).

60. **Q.** Are there then three Gods?
A. No. There is only One God, but in three "Persons": the Father, the Son, and the Holy Spirit. Christians call this the doctrine of the Holy Trinity, and it is a mystery which we cannot fully understand with our finite minds. We can understand partially through various analogies, like water, steam, and ice, or the three dimensions. Or we can find a suggestion in the sun sending out its visible light to the earth, together with all the invisible rays and warmth which make life possible.

61. **Q.** Can we come to know and experience God as the Holy Trinity?
A. Yes. The teaching about the Holy Trinity arises from the experience of millions of ordinary Christians, who believe in God, our Heavenly Creator, who made us all and watches over us; Jesus of Nazareth, as Christ, the Mes-

siah, showing God's nature; and the Holy Spirit within and among us, bringing us into communion with Christ, and giving us the power to know God's will and to do it.

62. **Q.** Why do we call the Bible, or the Holy Scriptures, the Word of God?
A. We call the Holy Scriptures the Word of God because we believe God inspired their human authors and because God still speaks to us through their words (2 Tim. 3:15-16; 2 Pet. 1:21; BCP, p. 853).

63. **Q.** How should we read the Bible?
A. It is important to read a little of the Bible every day. We should read it with prayer and try to find what God is saying to us through it here and now, and how we can make our lives an offering to God and others. In order to read different parts of the Bible in an orderly way, we should follow a plan of daily readings such as the "Daily Office Lectionary" (BCP, pp. 936-995) or *Forward Day by Day*.

64. **Q.** Are all parts of the Bible of the same value?
A. No. Parts of the Old Testament have been superseded by the New, and the old Jewish laws are not obligatory for Christians, although we may learn much from the principles behind them. We must also remember that the social situation in which we live is very different from what it was at the time the Bible was written. God's truth, love, and justice never change; "Jesus Christ is the same yesterday, today, and forever" (Heb. 13:8). But the world changes, and we must learn to show God's love in our lives where we are.

65. **Q.** Should every word of the Bible be understood literally?
A. No. Much of the Bible is poetic language. When Christ said, "I am the door" (Jn. 10:7), he was not speaking literally, of course. The creation account in Genesis 1 should

not be understood as a scientific explanation of the origin of the universe, but a poetic expression of the religious truth that God made all things. The important thing in the Bible is what God has done and is doing for us, and what God is saying to us today, not the historical details or particular verbal expressions.

66. **Q.** Should we rely on ourseleves alone to understand the Bible?
A. We should certainly read the Bible ourselves, but it is good to have help from other persons and books to understand it rightly. There are many things in the Bible no ordinary person could possibly understand without the help of others, nor can we always see what doctrines they lead to. History has shown many times that when people adopt "private" interpretations of the Bible, they make serious errors and lead others into them.

67. **Q.** Who, then, teaches us how to interpret the Bible rightly?
A. The Church. The Holy Spirit, through the Church, guides readers of the Bible today, just as the Holy Spirit guided the authors of the Holy Scriptures in the past. Through the ages people in the Church have read the Bible, and under the guidance of the Holy Spirit have learned to interpret it, to teach its truths, and to correct the errors of those who read it wrongly. The Church's Creeds enshrine the essential truths of Scripture. The Church stands as interpreter and guardian of the Scripture.

68. **Q.** Which came first, the Church or the Bible?
A. The Christian Church existed for many years before any part of the New Testament was written; and Israel, which was the "Church" of the Old Covenant, existed long before the Old Testament was put in writing. It was the Church, led by the Holy Spirit, which decided which

writings were to be included in the Holy Scriptures, and which were not. God's revelation called the Church into being and the record of that revelation was recorded, sifted, and selected by the Church. Neither the Church nor the Bible is absolute, for both are under God. God gave the Bible through the Church, but since it is God's Word, the Church and its traditions are judged and defined by "God's Word written."

69. **Q.** Does not God reveal truth directly to individuals apart from the Church or the Bible?

A. We believe that God speaks to us throughout our lives, especially in prayer. We treasure these moments, these "conversations" with God. We thank God that we were endowed with reason and the ability to seek for the truth, and with conscience to distinguish between good and evil. We recognize that many have experienced the Holy Spirit's power in their lives. But in humility we should also confess that our reason can be distorted by pride, self-centeredness, and sin, and that our consciences may be warped by the prejudices and corruptions of the societies in which we live. For these reasons we should always avail ourselves of the guidance God gives us through the Holy Scriptures and the Church as standards by which to compare, test, and sort out our personal experiences.

Questions to Think About—II

a. If we didn't have the Bible, how much would we know about God, Christ, the Holy Spirit, and the meaning of life?
b. If the Gospels told us only about the teaching of Jesus, would that be enough?
c. Would it be all right to read just the New Testament and not the Old?
d. What should be our attitude to the scriptures of other religions?

III   The Church

70. **Q.** What is the Church?
A. The Church is the community of the New Covenant, the fellowship of all Christians, in all ages, founded by Jesus Christ and empowered by the Holy Spirit to carry on the work of Christ as his representative. We may sometimes speak of a church building, or of a particular group of Christians, as a "church," but *the* Church, in the real sense, is the whole people of God, called by God to do God's work in the world (BCP, p. 854).

71. **Q.** How is the Church described in the Bible?
A. The Church is those who are "called out," (*ecclesia* in Greek) to be "the body of Christ," of which Jesus Christ is the head, and all baptized Christians are the members (1 Cor. 12:27; Eph. 4:15; Col. 1:18). It is built on the foundation of the apostles and the prophets (Eph. 2:20. See also BCP, p. 854.)

72. **Q.** With what great treasures is the Church entrusted?
A. The Church is entrusted with the Holy Scriptures, the Sacraments, the Creeds, and the Ministry. It is the responsibility of the Church to preserve these and to present them to all people.

73. **Q.** What is the purpose or mission of the Church?
A. The mission of the Church is to restore all people to unity with God and each other in Christ (BCP, p. 855). In doing this the Church is carrying on Christ's work of reconciliation bringing all people to a knowledge of God, leading them into the way of salvation.

74. **Q.** What is salvation?
A. Salvation (from *salus,* health or wholeness) means to be freed by Christ from the power of sin and death, and

to enter into the new life of love, service, and joy, in communion with God, by faith in Christ, and through the grace and power of the Holy Spirit (Mt. 1:21; Jn. 3:16; 10:10; Acts 4:12; Rom. 8:2; 2 Cor. 5:17).

75. **Q.** What are the functions of the Church in the world?
A. The functions of the church in the world are: proclamation or witness (*kerygma*); service or ministry (*diakonia*); and fellowship or communion (*koinonia*). The Church is not a static institution, but a dynamic fellowship of the witnessing servants of Christ in God's world.

76. **Q.** Is the Church only for good people?
A. No. If the Church were only for good people, there would be no one in it. Jesus said, "I came not to call the righteous, but sinners to repentance" (Lk. 5:32). Christians acknowledge that they, like all other people, are sinners. Of course, we are called to make our lives better with God's help, and we certainly hope for improvement. We should never be self-satisfied with the way we are nor think that we are really good. The Church is not a club for hypocrites who think they are perfect, but rather like a hospital where people who know they are sick come to be healed ("saved") by the great Physician of souls (Lk. 5:31; 18:9-14).

77. **Q.** Can we be saved outside the Church?
A. God can save people under any conditions, of course (Lk. 23:39-43), but to ignore the means of grace which Christ has entrusted to the Church would seem to be directly opposed to his purposes. A drowning man might possibly be washed ashore by holding onto a piece of wood, but if a lifeboat should come along, he would be foolish not to get into it.

78. **Q.** What great problem did the early Church face in the apostolic age?

A. The Church had to decide whether or not it was necessary for Christian converts, especially gentiles, to obey all the Jewish laws of the Old Testament (Acts 15:5). The Church decided, under the guidance of the Holy Spirit, that Christians were not bound to obey all the laws of the Old Testament, but should put their faith in Christ and follow his example of love to God and neighbor, which, as he said, is the fulfillment of all the Law and the Prophets (Mt. 22:37-40; Acts 15). St. Paul, especially, taught us that we could not be saved by obedience to the Law, but only through faith in Christ, and that the Law could actually become a hindrance to us when it did not serve the ends of justice (Rom. 7:10; Gal. 2:16, 3:24).

79. **Q.** What was the great commission which Christ gave to his disciples to carry on his work, and what promise did he give them?

A. "Go, therefore, and make disciples of all nations, baptizing them in the name of the Father, and of the Son, and of the Holy Spirit, teaching them to observe all that I have commanded you; and lo, I am with you always, to the close of the age" (Mt. 28:19-20).

80. **Q.** How was it possible for Christ to be with the disciples always?

A. Through the Holy Spirit, Christ is with all Christians in his Church (Jn. 14:15-26).

81. **Q.** How did the apostles whom Jesus chose (Mt. 10:2) perpetuate their ministry and provide successors?

A. The apostles ordained others with the laying on of hands and prayer under the guidance of the Holy Spirit (Acts 13:2-3; 1 Tim. 2:7). These in turn, ordained others, whom we call bishops, to be their successors (2 Tim. 1:6; 2:2; Titus 1:5). The apostles also ordained elders (or presbyters) in the various churches (Acts 14:23; Titus 1:5), and deacons to serve with them (Acts 6).

82. **Q.** How did the early Church define its faith?
    A. In the first four great Church councils, called because of divisions, and especially in the Council of Nicea (325 AD), a *creed* (or formal statement of belief—from the Latin *credo,* I believe) was agreed upon. This was revised slightly in subsequent councils, receiving its final form at the Council of Chalcedon in 451. It is called the Nicene Creed (BCP, pp. 326-328, 358-359). The Nicene Creed is the creed of the universal Church and is used frequently at the Eucharist (BCP, p. 852).

83. **Q.** What is the Apostles' Creed?
    A. The Apostles' Creed is the ancient creed of Baptism; it is used in the Church's daily worship to recall our baptismal covenant (BCP, pp. 53-54, 66, 96, 120, 852).

84. **Q.** What is the Athanasian Creed?
    A. The Athanasian Creed is a historic document proclaiming the nature of the Incarnation and of God as Trinity (BCP, pp. 852, 864-865). These creeds agree at all important points. In them the Church affirms the heart of the faith and the most important truths of the Bible.

(For more about the Church, see Chapters IV and IX.)

Questions to Think About—III

a. **Could we have the Bible without the Church?**
b. **How did you first find out about God and Jesus Christ?**
c. **Is it possible to be a Christian but to refuse to join a church?**

IV   The Creeds

85. **Q.** What are the creeds?
    A. The creeds of the Church are affirmations of faith in God and of thanksgiving and confidence in what God has done, is doing, and will do. They are a recital of the mighty acts of God, not a listing of abstract doctrinal statements about God which have to be intellectually accepted.

86. **Q.** Into what three parts is the Nicene Creed divided?
    A. The Nicene Creed is divided into three main parts, expressing our faith in God the Father, God the Son, and God the Holy Spirit—the One Triune God.

87. **Q.** How do we affirm our faith in God the Father in the Nicene Creed?
    A. "We believe in one God, the Father, the Almighty, maker of heaven and earth, of all that is, seen and unseen" (BCP, p. 358).

88. **Q.** What do we mean when we say, "We believe"?
    A. We mean that we trust and have complete confidence in God, as we might in some person whom we love and respect and on whom we depend entirely, as small children depend on their parents. It means that we are willing to base our whole lives on this trusting relationship, and that we find in God the meaning and purpose for which we live.

89. **Q.** Why do we call God "Father"?
    A. Although God is transcendent and omnipotent, and in one sense totally different from us, yet God loves us and has made us in his own image, and God is closer to us than any person on this earth. Therefore we are taught by Christ to call God "our Father" and to think

of ourselves as God's children (Mt. 6:9, 32; see also Q. 40).

90. **Q.** Does this mean we believe in a "masculine" God?
A. No. Jesus was expressing the truth of our relationship to God in symbolic language. Because of the reality of Jewish society at that time, it was natural to use "Father," indicating authority and power as well as love, but Genesis 1:27 tells us that both male and female were created in God's image, as persons in relationship.

91. **Q.** What do we mean by saying that God is the creator of things "unseen"?
A. We believe that, besides the physical world which we can see or find out about with scientific instruments, there is also a spiritual world which God created too. We cannot know very much about it through physical sensation, but the Bible speaks of angels and other spiritual beings created by God (Lk. 1:26; 2:9-15; Col. 1:16-17; Heb. 1:14). There is, of course, the whole "world of the spirit," including such things as love, faith, truth, and goodness, which are partly invisible, and perhaps these may also be thought of as the "invisible things" which God has created here and in the kingdom of heaven.

92. **Q.** How do we affirm our faith in God the Son in the Nicene Creed?
A. "We believe in one Lord, Jesus Christ, the only Son of God, eternally begotten of the Father, God from God, Light from Light, true God from true God, begotten, not made, of one Being with the Father. Through him all things were made. For us and for our salvation he came down from heaven: by the power of the Holy Spirit he became incarnate from the Virgin Mary, and was made man. For our sake we was crucified under Pontius Pilate; he suffered death and was buried. On the third day he

rose again in accordance with the Scriptures; he ascended into heaven and is seated at the right hand of the Father. He will come again in glory to judge the living and the dead, and his kingdom will have no end" (BCP, p. 358).

93. **Q.** What do we mean when we say that Jesus is "the only Son of God"?

A. We mean that Jesus is the only perfect image of the Father, and shows us the nature of God (BCP, p. 849). The Father and the Son are one God, and in all things equal, eternal, and infinite. And yet they are, although of one "Being" or "Substance," two different "Persons," bound together by love as of parent and child. We ourselves are called "children of God," but that is because God, who created us, has in love adopted us as children in the new creation, through the grace of our Lord Jesus Christ.

94. **Q.** What do we mean when we say that by the power of the Holy Spirit Jesus became incarnate from the Virgin Mary?

A. We mean that by God's own act, his divine Son received our human nature from the Virgin Mary, his mother. The divine Son became human, so that in him human beings might be adopted as children of God, and be made heirs of God's kingdom (BCP, pp. 849-50, Jn. 1:14; Gal. 4:4-7; Col. 1:19; 2:9; see also Questions 43-49).

95. **Q.** What is the great importance of Jesus' suffering and death?

A. By his obedience, even to suffering and death, Jesus made the perfect offering which we could not make; in him we are freed from the power of sin and reconciled to God (BCP, p. 850).

96. **Q.** What is the significance of Jesus' resurrection?
A. By his resurrection, Jesus overcame death and opened for us the way to eternal life (BCP, p. 850).

97. **Q.** What do we mean when we say that Jesus "descended to the dead" in the Apostles' Creed?
A. We mean that Jesus went to the departed and offered them also the benefits of redemption (BCP, p. 850). We cannot know the precise meaning of this, but it emphasizes the fact that Christ's death was a real death, not just a pretense. It also stresses the universality of Christ's redemption. In 1 Peter 3:19 and 4:6, it is written that Christ "went and preached to the spirits in prison . . . even to the dead," and so we believe that God's love and redemption are offered to all people of all ages.

98. **Q.** What do we mean when we say that Christ "ascended into heaven and is seated at the right hand of the Father"?
A. We mean that Jesus took our human nature into heaven where he now reigns with the Father and intercedes for us (BCP, p. 850). This is metaphorical language to express something which we cannot really imagine. The disciples saw Jesus ascend, but they did not see him enter heaven (Acts 1:9). Heaven is not a physical place "up there," but is the spiritual presence of God. When we say that Christ is "at the right hand of the Father," we mean that Christ is with God in the closest possible way. When we say that Christ "is seated," we mean that he reigns as a king, and that he has completed his saving work as our great high priest, having offered the perfect sacrifice of his life once and for all (Lk. 24:51; Acts 1:9; Rom. 8:34; Col. 3:1; Heb. 10:12).

99. **Q.** What do we mean by saying that Christ "will come again in glory"?
A. The same Jesus who was once born in a stable and

lived on earth as a carpenter and rabbi, the friend of the poor and despised, who was executed with thieves on a cross, and who rose and ascended to the Father, will return to bring earthly history to an end and to fulfill all the purposes of God (Jn. 14:3; Acts 1:11; Col. 3:4; 1 Jn. 3:2).

100.   **Q.** What do we mean by saying that Christ will "judge the living and the dead"?
A. The lives which we live on this earth, and the faith and love we live by are directly connected to our future lives. Christ, who is our merciful Savior and just judge, will judge us and all people according to our lives, our true repentence, and our faith (Mt. 25:31-46; Rom. 14:10-12; 2 Cor. 5:10; 2 Tim. 4:1).

101.   **Q.** What do we mean when we say, "His kingdom will have no end"?
A. Christ's "kingdom" is not so much to be thought of as a place, but as Christ's sovereignty or rule as king. The "kingdom" is Christ's love and justice working unhindered in all things, and this rule will be everywhere and eternal (Lk. 1:33; Heb. 1:8; Rev. 11:15).

102. **Q.** How do we affirm our faith in God the Holy Spirit in the Nicene Creed?
A. "We believe in the Holy Spirit, the Lord, the giver of life, who proceeds from the Father and the Son. With the Father and the Son he is worshiped and glorified. He has spoken through the Prophets" (BCP, p. 359).

103. **Q.** Who is the Holy Spirit?
A. The Holy Spirit is the Third Person of the Trinity, God at work in the world and in the Church even now (BCP, p. 852). We may think of our Lord, the Holy Spirit, as God dwelling in us and the upholder of all things, in whom "we live and move and have our being" (Acts 17:28). The

Holy Spirit abides in our hearts, enlightens our consciences, informs our reason, and brings us into spiritual fellowship with God and all people. By the grace of the Holy Spirit we pray, receive power from on high, and are given faith to know God the Father and Jesus Christ.

104. **Q.** Why is the Holy Spirit called "the giver of life"?
A. The Holy Spirit gives to all creation both the physical, biological life which we share with all living creatures, and also the spiritual life which comes from God, and which makes us heirs and fellow-citizens of the kingdom of heaven (Rom. 8:13-17). The Holy Spirit infused the breath of life at the start of creation (Gen. 1:2; 2:7), and was the agent through whom new life entered the world in Jesus Christ and abides in the Church (Lk. 1:35; 3:22; 4:1, 14, 18-21; Acts 2). Therefore the Holy Spirit is called "the giver of life." Truth, beauty, goodness, love, liberty, harmony, and holiness are the sacred marks or gifts of the Holy Spirit in creation (see also Questions 55-59).

105. **Q.** Why do we say the Holy Spirit "has spoken through the Prophets" in the Nicene Creed?
A. We believe that the Holy Spirit inspired the prophets of the Old Testament to speak and to write. We may say the same thing of all the writers of the Bible. We also believe that the Holy Spirit has continued to inspire faithful people of the Church in all ages, and that in this age the Holy Spirit enlightens the hearts and minds of countless teachers, writers, philosophers, scientists, artists, and leaders both within and without the Church (Isa. 61:1; 2 Tim. 3:16; Heb. 1:1-2; 2 Pet. 1:21).

106. **Q.** How do we recognize the presence of the Holy Spirit in our lives?
A. We recognize the presence of the Holy Spirit in our lives when we confess Jesus Christ as Lord and are brought into love and harmony with God, with ourselves, our neighbors, and all creation (BCP, p. 852).

107. **Q.** What other things do we say that we believe in the Nicene Creed?

A. "We believe in one holy catholic and apostolic Church. We acknowledge one baptism for the forgiveness of sins. We look for the resurrection of the dead, and the life of the world to come. Amen" (BCP, p. 358).

108. **Q.** Why is the Church described as *one?*

A. The Church is one, because it is one Body, under one Head, our Lord Jesus Christ (BCP, p. 854).

109. **Q.** How can we say that the Church is one if there are many denominations?

A. The Church is one because, even though there are many denominations as a result of our sins and imperfect faith and understanding, it is one body in Christ, under his lordship. We all believe in one God, are saved by one savior, Jesus Christ, are guided by the same Holy Spirit, receive the same baptism, and read the same Bible. We are all baptized, not in particular churches, but into the one Church of Jesus Christ. Though there are human divisions among us, our unity is much more important than our differences. Unity is both God's gift to the Church and his will for the churches; thus we must work and pray that we may draw closer together as we come nearer to Christ (Jn. 17:21; 1 Cor. 12:4-6, 11-13; Eph. 4:3-6).

110. **Q.** Why is the Church described as *holy* in the Nicene Creed?

A. The Church is holy, because the Holy Spirit dwells in it, consecrates its members, and guides them to do God's work (BCP, p. 854). This does not mean that the Church is perfect as it exists on earth, but it does mean that it is God's representative in this world and the chief channel of God's grace (Eph. 5:27; 1 Pet. 2:9).

111. **Q.** Why is the church described as *catholic* in the Nicene Creed?

A. The Church is catholic, because it proclaims the whole Faith to all people, to the end of time (BCP, p. 854). It is universal, for all people, in all places, in all times. A "church" which is a class "church," or for only one race or one nation, or which is not missionary, is not the catholic Church of God, for that would be a contradiction of its divine commission (Mt. 28:19). In the unhappily divided Church of today, no denomination can claim exclusive right to the word "catholic," and we must all recognize that any particular branch is only a part of Christ's one holy catholic Church.

112. **Q.** Why is the Church described as *apostolic* in the Nicene Creed?
A. The Church is apostolic, because it continues the teaching and fellowship of the apostles and is sent to carry out Christ's mission to all people (BCP, p. 854). It is not a new human organization, but the same divine institution "built upon the foundation of the apostles" (Eph. 2:20; Jn. 20:19-22).

113. **Q.** What is the "one baptism for the forgiveness of sins"?
A. In baptism we receive new birth in the Holy Spirit, and are adopted into the one, universal family of the Church as children of God, members of Christ, and inheritors of the kingdom of heaven. In baptism we receive the washing away or forgiveness of sins and the beginning of the transformation of our sinful nature by the power of the Holy Spirit, so that we can become more and more like Jesus, the pattern for our lives. It is *one* baptism because the Church is one, and baptism is not repeated, even though a person might change from one denomination to another (Jn. 3:5; Rom. 6:3-11; Eph. 4:5; see also Chapter VII).

114. **Q.** What does "the resurrection of the dead" mean?
A. For Christ, death on the cross was not the end. "On

the third day he rose again." But neither was his life after the resurrection merely a continuation of his life on earth. It had a new quality of spiritual power and glory. For us, too, death is not the end, but through the power of the Holy Spirit, and because of the victory of Christ, we also look forward to the resurrection, when we shall be with Christ in his glory. (Jn. 5:25-29; 1 Cor. 15; Phil. 3:20-21).

115. **Q.** What does "the resurrection of the body" in the Apostles' Creed mean?

A. It has the same meaning as the Nicene Creed. The word, "body," does not mean our earthly, physical flesh, but it does mean that our full selves, with all that makes up our personality, will be redeemed and will have continuity in the future life. No person whom Christ has redeemed will lose his or her individual identity. We will not be disembodied, nonpersonal spirits merged indistiguishably in an ocean of being, but we will be our true selves for the first time, more fully alive than ever before (1 Cor. 15:35-44; 1 Jn. 3:2). The Bible and the creeds do not speak of "the immortality of the soul" as inherent in ourselves; resurrection is the gift of God through Jesus Christ our Lord.

116. **Q.** What is "the life of the world to come" or "the life everlasting"?

A. By everlasting life, we mean a new existence, in which we are united with all the people of God, in the joy of fully knowing and loving God and each other (BCP, p. 862). We cannot imagine what the future life will be, but we do know that Jesus promised that there is a place for each of us in his Father's house (Jn. 14:2), and that we shall be with him (14:3). It is enough to know that we will be with God, for there is no better place to be. This is the highest blessing and ultimate happiness. The quality of that life will be love, joy, and peace. Even here on earth we can have a foretaste of this eternal life through Christ in his kingdom, a life of continual growth in his love and service (Jn. 17:3; Rom. 6:22-23). Yet we must not forget that the denial of Christ and his way of love may condemn us to separation from God, for it may make us incapable of experiencing the joy and peace of a life whose quality is self-giving love (Mt. 25:31-46; Lk. 12:15-21; Jn. 5:21-29).

117. **Q.** What is "the communion of saints" in the Apostles' Creed?

A. The communion of saints is the whole family of God, the living and the dead, those whom we love and those whom we hurt, bound together in Christ by sacrament, prayer, and praise (BCP, p. 862). In the New Testament, the word "saints" means those who are made holy, or set apart, and it refers to all Christians (Rom. 1:7; 1 Cor. 1:2). This does not mean that they are always morally better or more pure than others, but that through Christ they have received the gift of the Holy Spirit and are striving to press on to the likeness of Christ, no matter how far from the goal they may be (Phil. 3:12-14). We and all Christians of all ages, past, present, and future, belong to the fellowship of those who love the Lord Jesus, and are bound together with him and with each other by the Holy Spirit into the communion of Christ's followers in all places, both on this earth and in the world to come (Eph. 2:19; 4:15-16; 2 Cor. 13:14).

118. **Q.** Is Christian faith just a matter of understanding the creeds and accepting the truth of their statements?

A. No. Christian faith is much more than mere assent to a set of propositions. Our faith is a personal relationship of trust in God and of grateful loyalty to God. It involves making a personal commitment of ourselves to God, and dedicating our will and all our powers to God as our highest good. The creeds help us to know God's nature, and they remind us of what God has done for us. But truly to know and to trust in God is not simply a question

43

of understanding with the mind. It is to love God with our whole being. This is only possible because God in Christ has first sought us out, and has given us grace through the Holy Spirit who makes faith possible. By prayer, by reading the Bible, and by the means given to us in the Church and sacraments, we can come to know God more and more. Only by God's grace can we love, trust, and believe in God (Jn. 15:16; Eph. 2:7-8; 1 Jn. 4:10).

119. **Q.** What is grace?

A. Grace is God's favor toward us, unearned and undeserved. By grace God forgives our sins, enlightens our minds, stirs our hearts, and strengthens our wills (BCP, p. 858). Grace is the power, help, and guidance of the Holy Spirit, which is given to us to overcome all that would separate us from God.

120. **Q.** Is faith necessary for salvation?

A. Yes. Faith is essential, as Ephesians 2:8 tells us: "For by grace you have been saved through faith; and this is not your own doing, it is the gift of God."

Questions to Think About—IV

a. Some people say, "It doesn't matter what you believe, as long as you believe something and are true to it." What do you think of that?
b. If you led "a good life," would your beliefs be of any importance?
c. Isn't the Nicene Creed out of date, and don't we need a modern revision?

V   The Ethic of Love

121.   **Q.** If we are saved "by grace through faith," do our actions have any importance?

A. Yes. What we believe, what we say, and what we do are all important. Our actions should reflect our faith (James 2:17). Jesus said, "Not every one who says to me, Lord, Lord, shall enter into the kingdom of heaven, but he who does the will of my Father who is in heaven" (Mt. 7:21). Since we have free will and reason, we are responsible for our actions and have to make many choices and decisions every day. Our decisions and our actions should be according to our faith and should show our thanksgiving and our love to God (Deut. 30:15, 19-20).

122.   **Q.** Did Jesus give us any principle which should be the basis of our ethical decisions?

A. Yes. Jesus taught us in words and in his own life that all our decisions and actions should be based on the principle of love (Jn. 13:34). Since we believe in God, who is love (1 Jn. 4:16), and in Christ, who is the incarnation and manifestation of love, we know that all our thoughts, words, and deeds should reflect this love (1 Jn. 4:7-11). The Christian ethic proceeds from thanksgiving to God for all God's love, and produces a response of love on our part (Eph. 5:1-2).

123.   **Q.** What is Christian love?

A. Christian love is the love with which God loves us, and it is our reflection of that love, in loving God and others. It is not just a feeling, nor just affection, nor just liking a person. Christian love is a matter of the will, for we are commanded to love even those whom we do not particularly like. Christian love is a giving of ourselves to the other, whether God or a person, and desiring the best for that other (1 Cor. 13:4-7). It is self-sacrificing love rather than acquisitive or possessive love. It is genuine justice, rather than judgment. We can best see this love in Jesus Christ. (In older translations of the Bible this love is called "charity." In Greek it is called *agape*, pronounced ah-**gah**-pay.)

124. **Q.** What commandments did Christ give us?
A. Christ gave us the Two Great Commandments, or Summary of the Law: "You shall love the Lord your God with all your heart, with all your soul, and with all your mind. This is the first and the great commandment. And the second is like it: You shall love your neighbor as yourself" (BCP, p. 851). He also said, "On these two commandments depend all the law and the prophets" (Mt. 22:37-40).

125. **Q.** What did Jesus mean by "the law and the prophets"?
A. By "the law and the prophets" Jesus meant the Old Testament and God's revelation contained in it. In Jesus' words, these two commandments, which are found in Deuteronomy 6:5 and Leviticus 19:18, summarize all the ethical and moral teachings of the Old Testament and give them their highest meaning.

126. **Q.** What was the most important set of laws in the Old Testament by which God's will for Israel was shown?
A. There were many laws in the Old Testament, but God's will for Israel was shown most clearly in the Ten Commandments or Decalogue (BCP, p. 847), as set forth in Exodus 20:1-17.

127. **Q.** Should Christians obey all the laws of the Old Testament?
A. Many of the Old Testament laws concerned Sabbath observance, the ritual of the Temple in Jerusalem, whether things were ceremonially "clean" or "unclean,"

46

and customs which are no longer relevant today. Jesus indicated that many of these outward laws were no longer binding on his followers (Mk. 7:14-23). Even in Old Testament times the prophets taught that "to do jutice, and to love kindness" were more important than carrying out ritual observances (Mic. 6:8), and Jeremiah prophesied that God would make a new covenant and would write the law in our hearts (Jer. 31:31-33). We believe that this prophecy was fulfilled in Jesus Christ and in the gift of the Holy Spirit at Pentecost. For us, therefore, the most important thing is to respond to God's love shown to us in Christ by following the Summary of the Law, to love God and to love our neighbors.

128. **Q.** How can we obey the First Great Commandment, to love God?

A. As we come to know God well, we can love God as we love a person whom we respect very much, or a parent who is always loving and good and who calls forth the best from us. Loving God involves faith, trust, obedience, and the giving of our ourselves to God. Love means giving first priority to serving God, never putting anything in the way of that love. It involves the will and loving *deeds*. It is not just a feeling or emotion. To help us in loving God whom we cannot see, the first four of the Ten Commandments are an excellent guide. The first teaches that we must love and obey God and bring others to know him, and that we must never let any worldly thing, ambition, or desire become the center of our lives or take the place of God (Ex. 20:2-3; Job 31:24-28; Mt. 6:24, 33). The second also warns us against putting anything else in the place of God. The third reminds us that we must show our respect and devotion to our Lord God in our thoughts, words and deeds. The fourth tells us that we must set aside regular times for worship, prayer, and the study of God's ways and word (BCP, p. 847).

47

129. **Q.** What is the meaning of "neighbor" in the Second Great Commandment?

A. Jesus answered this question with the Parable of the Good Samaritan (Lk. 10:29-37). My neighbor is not the person whom I choose, but the one whom God gives to me to be my neighbor, of whatever class, or race, or position, but especially those in need of help. Today, with fast travel and communication, all people throughout the world are, in a new sense, our neighbors, and to some degree we have a responsibility to all. If we live in a society which insulates us, through selfish separation from those who have need, then it is our duty to try to break down this separation and to go out and seek our neighbors in order to show love and seek justice for them.

130. **Q.** How can we fulfill our Lord's Second Great Commandment, "You shall love your neighbor as yourself"?

A. We should love all people, because they are our brothers and sisters for whom Christ died. Jesus said, "As you did it to one of the least of these my brethren, you did it to me" (Mt. 25:40). When we show our love to others by our kindness, friendliness, and helpfulness, we are doing it as though to Christ. This commandment implies that we should care for ourselves in body, mind, and spirit in order to show our love to others. Jesus also gave us what has been called the Golden Rule, "to do to other people as we wish them to do to us" (BCP, p. 848, Lk. 6:31). All of us from birth have a tendency toward self-centeredness, and as we grow older, toward selfishness and pride. These things work against love, and to overcome them we need God's help. In trying to keep the commandment to love our neighbors, the last six of the Ten Commandments form a good guide. Being mainly negative prohibitions, they are not sufficient in themselves, but since we are basically self-centered, we need them as reminders and checks. As

Christians we can interpret them positively as Christ has taught us. If we understand the commandments in this way, they can help us to find the structure and expression for our love. The fifth commandment, "Honor your father and mother," teaches us "To love, honor, and help our parents and family; to honor those in authority, and to meet their just demands" (Ex. 20:12; BCP, p. 848). The sixth, "You shall not commit murder," teaches us "To show respect for the life God has given us; to work and pray for peace, to bear no malice, prejudice, or hatred in our hearts; and to be kind to all the creatures of God" (Ex. 20:13; Mt. 5:22; I Jn. 3:15-18; BCP, p. 848). The seventh, "You shall not commit adultery," teaches us "To use our bodily desires as God intended," and to treat the God-given institutions of marriage and the family with reverence and faithfulness (Ex. 20:14; Mk. 10:9; 1 Cor. 6:18-20; BCP, p. 848). The eighth, "You shall not steal," teaches us "To be honest and fair in our dealings; to seek justice, freedom, and the necessities of life for all people; and to use our talents and possessions as ones who must answer for them to God" (Ex. 20:15; Eph. 4:28; James 5:4; BCP, p. 848). The ninth, "You shall not bear false witness," teaches us "To speak the truth, and not to mislead others by our silence" (Ex. 20:16; Eph. 4:15, 29-32; BCP, p. 848). The tenth, "You shall not covet anything that belongs to your neighbor," teaches us "To resist temptations to envy, greed, and jealousy; to rejoice in other people's gifts and graces; and to do our duty for the love of God, who has called us into fellowship with him" (Ex. 20:17; 1 Tim. 6:6-10; BCP, p. 848).

131. **Q.** Is it enough for a Christian just to keep the Ten Commandments?

A. No. The Christian life of love is much more positive, and proceeds, not from a sense of duty and blind obedience to some absolute commandment, but from thanksgiving to God who loves us.

132. **Q.** What are the signs of life with the Holy Spirit?
A. St. Paul urges us to seek the fruit of the Holy Spirit, the nine gifts which are marks of the Christian life: love, joy, peace, patience, kindness, goodness, faithfulness, gentleness, self-control" (Gal. 5:22).

133. **Q.** Should a Christian become involved in politics, and civic, social, or economic problems?
A. We are not merely isolated individuals, but members of Christ's Church and persons living in families, communities, and nations, and we should try to make these better through corporate means, working with others within and without the church, as well as through individual effort. Environment has a great influence on character, and it is the work of love to try to improve it. One person, working alone, cannot educate the masses, heal all the sick, clean up the slums, provide jobs for all, reform a corrupt government, eliminate pollution, or correct social evils (although, with God's help, it is remarkable what even one dedicated person can do). But if we work with others, appeal to their consciences, and attack the system which contributes to the evil, we may accomplish a great deal. We need a social conscience, as well as a personal conscience. We need to apply the gospel to society as well as to individuals. Although the Church should not try to make decisions for its members on some controversial political matters, it ought to take the lead in working to meet human needs and attempting to attain peace and justice. The Church should also give guidance in the area of social ethics and be a model for individuals and governments. We need a vision and an ideal of the kingdom of God, of a community of justice and love, the family of God, of which we are all members and citizens, so that we can work for its fulfillment during our earthly pilgrimage (Isa. 65:17-25; Phil. 3:20; Heb. 11:10, 13-16; Rev. 21:1-4).

134. **Q.** Should we obey all the laws of the country in which we live and support the government?

A. The laws of Congress and of the states were passed with the consent of the representatives of the people, and in a democracy like ours, it is normally the duty of the people to obey those laws, and if they are not good, to go about changing them through democratic legislative procedures. We live under the protection of those laws and receive the benefits from them. Democracy is not in itself Christian and no government is perfect, but government is necessary because of our sin and self-centeredness in order to keep order and public safety. Even an imperfect government (if not absolutely evil) is better than anarchy (Rom. 13:1; 1 Pet. 2:12-17). There may, of course, be exceptions in extreme circumstances, as when a bad government commands something contrary to the Christian faith or human justice. Then it may be the duty of Christians to oppose the government even to the point of martyrdom (Acts 4:18-20; 5:25-29). When there is a bad law and a complacent society, it may sometimes be necessary to break that particular law in order to test it in court, or to demonstrate or petition in order to arouse others. But if we do so, we must make clear our support of the rule of law and our obedience to it, and we must be prepared to take responsibility for our civil disobedience and its consequences.

135. **Q.** What should the Christian attitude be toward alcoholic beverages?

A. There is no prohibition against these in the New Testament, and we know that wine was used by Christ in the Last Supper, as it is in the Holy Eucharist today (see also Jn. 2:1-11). What the New Testament does command is temperance, that we should not become drunk and lose our reason, which is the gift of God (Eph. 5:18). Drunkenness is a defilement of the body, which is the temple of the Holy Spirit (1 Cor. 6:19-20). It is a dangerous state, not only to the drinker, but to others, and often leads to tragedy and death. Drinking can become habit forming, ruining lives and whole families, and therefore, like the use of narcotics, it is much more dangerous than excess in some other things (Prov. 23:20- 21, 29-35). For these reasons many Christians abstain from alcohol completely, and for some, because of the nature of their work or other circumstances, total abstention may be the will of God. The Episcopal Church does not prohibit drinking, and many feel that, rightly used, alcoholic beverages can be a blessing for which we can thank God (Psalm 104:15). Certainly Christians should not drink when it would impair their work or endanger the lives of others. They should never allow themselves to get drunk or let drinking become a habit. They should be careful not to tempt others, weaker than themselves, causing them to become victims of alcohol (Rom. 14:21; 1 Cor. 8:13). It may also be possible for us to help those who have become victims of the disease of alcoholism to overcome it through such organizations as Alcoholics Anonymous.

136. **Q.** What about tobacco and narcotic drugs?
A. The Episcopal Church has no prohibition against smoking, but in view of the expense, danger to health, and cause of fires, it would at least seem best for those who have not acquired the habit to avoid taking it up, and for others to exercise moderation, if they cannot give it up completely, and to avoid causing discomfort and injury to others. Young people often start smoking and drinking because others are doing it, and because they think it will make them seem more grown up. Usually it doesn't and it is a much greater mark of maturity not to be pushed into something just because everyone else is doing it. When it comes to narcotic drugs, the problems are far more serious. It is sometimes said that smoking marijuana is not habit forming and has no harmful effects. Marijuana does entail a loss of judgment, however. The

damage other addictive drugs (narcotics, amphetamines, cocaine, etc.) are doing is enormous, not only in physical destruction, but also in the criminal and moral corruption which has devastated large parts of our society. In view of all this, is not total abstinence the mature Christian course?

137. **Q.** Is the individual conscience a sure guide to what is right and wrong?

A. Not always. The conscience has been called "reason informed by the Holy Spirit." Although we believe that the Holy Spirit will guide us, it is not always easy for the inexperienced Christian to "hear" the Holy Spirit. Our consciences have to be trained and educated in the true Christian life, but often they are more influenced and conditioned by the society and environment in which we live. Sometimes it is hard to decide what is the right course to take, and it is best to turn for advice to more experienced Christians, to the clergy, or to the teaching of our Church and its leaders. God often speaks to us and answers our prayers through people. One reason that education is so important is that it helps to give us an "informed conscience."

138. **Q.** What is the Christian position on racism?

A. Racial prejudice is a deadly sin, a denial of Christ and his love. It infects the individual and corrupts society with a host of other evils. The Church should be a place where universal love flourishes in personal relationships, and it should lead the fight against all forms of segregation, discrimination, and prejudice in society and in our individual lives (Psalm 133; Gal. 3:26-28; Eph. 4:1-6; Col. 3:10-11; Hymn 529).

139. **Q.** Are Christian ethics relevant to the modern technological world?

A. Yes. Christian ethics are the attempt to apply Christian love, not only to individual relationships, but to all social, economic, and political life. The social aspect of love is justice, which has been called, "love distributed among many neighbors." Many of the problems and issues of today were completely unknown in New Testament times, but the love which Christ showed and which he taught applies to today's problems as much as it did then. Now Christians must try to find in what ways love can be expressed in the face of such issues as the population explosion, environmental pollution, urbanization, changing life styles, automation, nuclear arms, the United Nations, and the welfare state. People are looking for ethical guidance in the fields of law, medicine, business, urban planning, and sexual morality. Because many of the issues are new, there is not always a Christian consensus, but we must nevertheless face them and try to deal with them using our reason under the guidance of the Holy Spirit in the light of Christian love (Jn. 16:7-15).

140. **Q.** Does the Church have an absolute and "official" answer for all moral questions?
A. No. The Church may put forth moral principles based on the revelation of the Bible, its own traditions, reason, and natural law, all ultimately based on the principle of Christian love. Within the Church, moral theologians may give guidance for individuals or groups in certain situations to help them make decisions. However, the Church cannot adopt an "official" position for some problems, because there are differences of opinion within the Church. We have to judge as God gives us light to see the truth. For example, the Church has not reached unanimous agreement on whether war is sometimes justified as a means to a good end. On a number of questions the Church's position has changed with changing circumstances and new understanding, guided, we believe, by the Holy Spirit. For centuries the Church countenanced slavery (which in the apostolic age was too deeply en-

trenched to be challenged), until the consciences of Christians were awakened. There are many areas in which the Church's teaching has changed, or is in the process of being reexamined, such as contraception, marriage laws, the position of women, capital punishment, euthanasia, abortion, and homosexuality. Since ethics concern the expression of love in human personal and social relationships, and since the circumstances in which we live change and our understanding changes, it is necessary for us always to be open to the guidance of the Holy Spirit and to try to find what the will of God is for us in our own times and places. Though Jesus Christ is "the same yesterday, today, and forever," we have a responsibility to minister his eternal love in the changing context of the times, places, and circumstances to which he calls us. We live not under absolute fixed laws and rules applied mechanically, but in dynamic, loving and forgiving personal relationships with our neighbors.

141. **Q.** Is it possible for us to be perfect?

A. No person, except Christ, has ever been perfect. Paul says, "None is righteous, no, not one" (Rom. 3:10). All are subject to the same temptations of pride and self-centeredness, and the experience of Paul is common to all: "For I do not do the good I want, but the evil I do not want is what I do" (Rom. 7:19). It is because we never realize perfect love, or do all that is required of us, that there is no possibility of *earning* our salvation by our own good works ("justifying" ourselves). Therefore we must trust in Christ and have faith in the mercy of God. But though we fall far short, our goal and standard can never be less than the perfection of Christ (Mt. 5:48). We are called to press forward to that goal by the power of the Holy Spirit, to gain victory over sin, and gradually to become more and more like Christ (Phil. 3:12- 14). Of ourselves alone this is impossible; but with the help of God the Holy Spirit, we live in hope and confidence (2 Cor.

3:18). This grace of the Holy Spirit working in us is called *sanctification* (1 Thess. 3:12-4:8).

142. **Q.** How can we obtain the help of the Holy Spirit for our sanctification and to enable us to follow Christ?
A. The Holy Spirit is ready to help us at all times. By opening ourselves to the Holy Spirit, and by actively trying to know God's will and to do it, we can prepare the way for the Holy Spirit to work in us and help us to imitate the life of Christ. Seeking to know God's will is a part of prayer, and praying is one of the most important things we can do to make it possible for the Holy Spirit to sanctify us and fill our lives with God's love (Jn. 14:26; Rom. 8:26; Eph. 6:18; Phil. 4:6-7; 1 Thess. 5:16-25).

Questions to Think About—V

a. What is the relation between faith and love, between love and justice?
b. Are our actions and our characters merely the result of heredity and environment?
c. What does separation of Church and State mean?
d. What do you think a reasonable Christian position on some of the contemporary problems mentioned in Question 140 might be? Why? Are there some areas of life the Church has "no business" dealing with? Why?

VI   **Prayer**

143. **Q.** What is Prayer?

A. Prayer is responding to God, by thought and deed, with or without words (BCP, p. 856). Prayer can also be called "conversation" with God, in which we open our hearts and minds to God, and God speaks to us, hears, answers, and guides us. Through prayer we come to know God's will and are given power to conform to it. Prayer is "living with God."

144. **Q.** What is Christian Prayer?

A. Christian prayer is response to God the Father, through Jesus Christ, in the power of the Holy Spirit (BCP, p. 856).

145. **Q.** What are the principal kinds of prayer?

A. The principal kinds of prayer are adoration, praise, thanksgiving, penitence, oblation, intercession, and petition (BCP, p. 856). Meditation is also a form of prayer.

146. **Q.** What is adoration?

A. Adoration is the lifting up of the heart and mind to God, asking nothing but to enjoy God's presence (BCP, p. 857). In our adoration we become consciously aware of God's presence and power around us and in us and in the depths of all things.

147. **Q.** Why are praise and thanksgiving necessary?

A. We praise God, not to obtain anything, but because God's Being draws praise from us. Thanksgiving is offered to God for all the blessing of this life, for our redemption, and for whatever else draws us closer to God (BCP, p. 857). When we praise God, we are thinking of who God is, of God's greatness and love, and of all that God has done for us, especially in our creation, life, and redemption in Jesus Christ. When we thank God we are acknowledging our complete dependence on God for all our material and spiritual blessings (Psalm 103:1-2; Eph. 5:19-20; 1 Thess. 5:17-18; BCP, pp. 95-96, 101, 836-41, passim).

148. **Q.** What is penitence?
A. In penitence, we confess our sins and make restitution where possible, with the intention to amend our lives (BCP, p. 857). God knows all our sins of thought, word, deed, and omission, but we cannot hope for God's forgiveness unless we acknowledge and repent of them. In confession and penitence we recognize our self-centeredness and pride, as well as the actual things we have done wrong which separate us from God, express our sorrow for them (contrition), and ask God's forgiveness, making a resolve to correct our faults with God's help. When we have done wrong to someone, we must also make restitution in some form, if it is at all possible, as well as expressing our apologies. If we admit our faults and ask for strength to overcome them, we can trust in God's mercy and hope for improvement (1 Jn. 1:8-9). If we hope for forgiveness, we also know that we must forgive others (Mt. 6:12, 14-15; BCP, pp. 41-2, 267-9, 360, 446-52).

149. **Q.** What is prayer of oblation?
A. Oblation is an offering, of ourselves, our lives and labors, in union with Christ, for the purposes of God (BCP, p. 857). This self-dedication is offered up to God in each Eucharist in association with Christ's sacrifice for us (see also BCP, p. 832, Prayer 61).

150. **Q.** What is intercession?
A. Intercession brings before God the needs of others (BCP, p. 857), and is a natural expression of our love for them (1 Tim. 2:1-4). Because we love others, we want to help them, and since we cannot always give them the help

they need, we ask God to help and bless them. Of course, if we do not give them the help that is within our power, our love and our prayer are not very sincere (James 2:15-16; 1 Jn. 3:17). In intercessory prayer we are not asking for a change in God's will or in the laws of the universe, but that we and those for whom we pray may be open to the help which God is giving to us, even before we pray (BCP, p. 394, Prayer 4). Intercessory prayer is important for our spiritual life and should be practiced every day (Eph. 6:18; James 5:16; BCP, pp. 810-835). To aid our memory we can make lists of those for whom we pray daily, weekly, or monthly.

151. **Q.** What is petition?
A. Petition is prayer for ourselves or something involving ourselves. "In petition, we present our own needs, that God's will may be done" (BCP, p. 857).

152. **Q.** Is it acceptable to ask for things for ourselves?
A. Christ himself taught us to ask God for things, both material and spiritual (Mt. 6:11; 7:7-11). In our prayers we should be completely honest, and not try to hide anything from God, who knows all that is in our hearts (Phil. 4:6). Some of the things we ask for may be necessities, and some not. We can pray for all of them; but we should also pray for a spirit of self-denial, if it is not God's will for us to have them. Petition should come after praise, thanksgiving, and intercession, and we should not let our prayers become cluttered with too many selfish requests. Petition also should include prayer for grace to do God's will, to love and forgive others, and for strength to resist temptation (Mt. 6:13).

153. **Q.** How does God answer our prayers?
A. God does not always answer our prayers in the way we want or think we want. Prayer is often answered through the words and actions of others. Sometimes

praying about something may bring about a psychological change within ourselves which enables us to accept it or deal with it. This, too, is one of God's ways of answering prayer, for God is the creator of our minds and can certainly work in and through our mental processes. Sometimes God says "No" to our requests or petitions, but this is still an answer (2 Cor. 12:7-10). God knows what is best for us much better than we do, and God's answer is not based on what we want at the moment, but on what is best for us and for others for our whole lives and for eternity. For this reason our prayers should always include Christ's prayer in Gethsemane: "Not what I will, but what thou wilt" (Mk. 14:36).

154. **Q.** What is meditation?
A. Meditation is thinking about the things of God and what they mean for our life. It may include all forms of prayer and range from wordless adoration to practical, hard thinking for ordinary day to day living and action in the light of God's love. Often it proceeds to an act of will, a resolution, or decision, or a nearer approach to God's love. Ideally, every Church service should have moments of silence for meditation. One way to practice meditation is to start with a passage from the Bible (perhaps our daily reading), and to ask ourselves what God is saying to us through it, here and now. In this way we are seeking to know God's will for us, and we may proceed to a new decision for action or self-dedication in the light of it. Writing down parts of our meditation may also be helpful.

155. **Q.** When should we pray?
A. All our work in God's name is a prayer, and prayer can be a part of all our activities. Prayer without action is insincere, and action without prayer often has no focus. Besides our prayers in church, we should make a habit of praying in the morning and evening (BCP, p. 136-143),

and before and after meals (BCP, p. 835). In addition we can pray before, during, and after work or study, or anything else we do. These may be very short prayers, only a word or two, like "Thank you, God," or "Help me, Lord," or "Bless and protect them," or "Give us strength to do this," or "Father, forgive me." We may just remember that God is with us or turn to ask God's will. As we dedicate and offer up ourselves and each thing we do to God, that action and our whole lives will become a prayer. Prayer is something we learn by doing.

156. **Q.** Is prayer a natural ability?
A. No. It is the Holy Spirit who gives us the desire and the ability to pray (Rom. 8:26-27). With the help of the Holy Spirit we try to make our prayers like those of Christ, in whose name we pray, and we try to make ourselves present to God and open to God's presence with us.

157. **Q.** Should we use our own words or a written form of prayer?
A. We should use both. We know that Jesus used both. In his private prayers, he spoke with the Father in his own words (Jn. 17). In our own private prayers, in praise, thanksgiving, confession, intercession, and petition, we should not hesitate to use our own words to frame thoughts. We also know that Christ used public, set forms of prayer, when he joined in the worship of the Temple or the synagogue (Lk. 4:16). He probably used the traditional blessings at meals, including the Last Supper, and at other times of the day, according to Jewish custom. Christ gave the disciples a form of prayer to use always, and to serve as a model for prayer, which we call "The Lord's Prayer." We believe that it is proper for us to use, not only the Lord's Prayer, but also other written prayers which have been formed under the guidance of the Holy Spirit in the Church.

158. **Q.** What is the Lord's Prayer, and where is it found?
A. The Lord's Prayer is the prayer which Jesus taught his disciples to use at all times. It is a model for all our prayers. It is found in two slightly different Greek translations (the original probably was in Aramaic) in Matthew 6:9-13 and Luke 11:2-4. (Traditional and contemporary English versions may be found together on page 364 of The Book of Common Prayer).

159. **Q.** What is the meaning of "Our Father who art in heaven"?
A. The God in whom we trust, to whom we pray, is perfect, omnipotent, and transcendent, and therefore, in one sense, infinitely separated from our finite and sinful nature. But at the same time, God is closer to us than any person on earth, closer than breathing, and loves us more than any human being we can ever know (1 Kings 8:27; Malachi 2:10; 1 Cor. 8:6; 1 Jn. 4:16).

160. **Q.** What is the meaning of "hallowed be thy Name"?
A. This is an expression of praise for the holiness of God, and at the same time a prayer that we and all people should praise God in our worship and in our lives, so that we may truly realize that God is the center and purpose of all. Those who pray this prayer sincerely should certainly keep the third commandment.

161. **Q.** What is the meaning of "thy kingdom come, thy will be done, on earth as it is in heaven"?
A. The Greek word for "kingdom" means "kingly rule." We are here praying that God's rule over all people may be realized, that each of us may be guided by God's love and not by selfish forces and the evil spirits of this world. Jesus said to his disciples, "The kingdom of God is within you" (Lk. 17:21), for in one sense God's rule has already begun in the Church and in the hearts and fellowship of those who believe. Yet this is only an imperfect realiza-

tion of God's reign, marred by our self-centeredness and lack of love. We pray that God's will may be done as we respond in loving obedience, so that some day the whole world will be filled with God's love and peace, and God's reign will be established forever (Mt. 7:21; 12:50; Phil. 2:12-13; Rev. 11:15).

162. **Q.** What is the meaning of "Give us this day our daily bread"?

A. This is a petition for the necessities of life. Christ taught us to pray for material things as well as spiritual (Mt. 7:7-11). God created the material world, and it is good (Gen. 1:31). God wills us to use it for our good and his glory (Gen. 1:28-29; 2:15, 19; 1 Tim. 4:3-5). Since we pray for "our bread," and not just "my bread," we should also be concerned for others, and especially for those who have none. It may be that God will answer this prayer through our actions in sharing and helping them to get bread, or whatever else they need. Christ is himself the Bread of Life (Jn. 6:48), and we may use this petition for spiritual grace as well.

163. **Q.** What is the meaning of "Forgive us our trespasses as we forgive those who trespass against us"?

A. Forgiveness is the heart of the gospel, because forgiveness is the breaking down of the separation between God and all people brought about by sin and self-centeredness. Only God can forgive us and bring about this reconciliation, and so we ask for God's forgiveness. But God has given us the ministry of reconciliation, and we must also forgive others (2 Cor. 5:18-19). We pray for reconciliation and peace, and for the forgiveness of our sins of thought, word, deed, and omission, for the sin of our human nature, and for the corporate sin of our society in which we share (Mt. 6:14-15; Eph. 4:31-32; Col. 3:13; 1 Jn. 1:8-10; BCP, p. 446-452).

164. **Q.** What is the meaning of "Lead us not into temptation but deliver us from evil"?

A. We ask that we may be spared all trials and temptations that are greater than we can overcome, all religious persecution, and suppression of rights and freedoms; and that with the trials which we must meet, we be given grace to conquer and rise to a richer understanding of God's love (1 Cor. 10:13; 2 Cor. 12:7-10). We pray that we may not ourselves be the occassion of temptation to others, that we may be delivered from the power of evil which tries to enslave us, and be, rather, the servants and instruments of God's love (Lk. 22:31-32; BCP, p. 833, Prayer 62).

165. **Q.** What is the meaning of "For Thine is the kingdom, and the power, and the glory, forever and ever"?

A. This is an offering of praise (a "doxology") and an expression of faith which the Church has made even in times of persecution, when all looked dark. It may have been added in the Church's worship, since it is not found in some of the most ancient Greek manuscripts of Matthew 6:13. We believe that God rules all things, will perfect and fulfill all that is imperfect now, and that God's kingdom will be forever (1 Chron. 29:11).

166. **Q.** What does "Amen" mean?

A. "Amen" is a Hebrew word and means "truly," or "so be it." In many prayers, when one person leads the prayer, the others can join in by saying "Amen" at the end, meaning that it is their prayer too. It is like a signature or seal, to show that these words which we use are not just words, but are a prayer in which we give ourselves to God with all our heart, mind, and body.

167. **Q.** Why do we use written prayers from The Book of Common Prayer or other books in our public worship, instead of using free prayers in our own words?

A. (1) We have Christ's teaching and example in the Lord's

Prayer, and in the Temple and synagogue worship in which he participated. (2) The Church, from the beginning, has used such forms of prayer and worship, not only the Lord's Prayer, but also psalms, hymns, the Aaronic blessing (Num. 6:22-26), and others which were used by the Jews. Traces of primitive liturgies are found in the New Testament (Rom. 10:9; 1 Cor. 11:23-27; Eph. 5:14; 1 Tim. 3:16; 2 Tim. 2: 11-13). (3) We believe the Holy Spirit inspired the Church to create forms which are universal, true to the faith, expressing the wisdom of the ages far more perfectly than any individual could invent. (4) By using written prayers, the whole congregation can pray together, and not just the minister, who himself may not always be inspired to find adequate words to express the prayers of the people. (5) These prayers create a unity and a fellowsip with other Christians in all places and ages who have used them in their worship.

168. **Q.** What are the contents of The Book of Common Prayer?
   A. The Book of Common Prayer is a book for the use of people and clergy in corporate worship, and consists of prayers, praises, and selections from the Bible to be used at different times and occasions. There are services for daily use, such as Morning and Evening Prayer, with lessons appointed so that, by following them, we may read almost the entire Bible in an orderly sequence during a two-year cycle (BCP, pp. 37-126; 934-995). There are orders of service for the administration of the sacraments, and to mark every major event of our lives: birth, growth, marriage, children, work, sickness, thanksgiving, sin, and death. The prayer book is based on the biblical and historical faith of the Church, and it meets our needs as children of God, living in today's world, with all its joys and problems.

169. **Q.** What was the origin of the various service books?
   A. From the time of the Early Church there has been a

need for order in Christian worship, so that all might worship harmoniously together, without the excesses of some offending the consciences of others (1 Cor. 14:26-33, 40). Traditions grew up, shaped by the Holy Spirit, and certain parts of scripture, for example Isaiah 6:3, or the words of Christ at the Last Supper (1 Cor. 11:23-26), became fixed parts of a growing liturgy, to which were added various prayers which developed out of the experience of the worshiping Church.

170. **Q.** When was The Book of Common Prayer written?
A. The latest revision of our prayer book was adopted in 1979, but the contents go back, in some cases, almost 3000 years. Some parts are taken directly from the Old and New Testaments and the Apocrypha. Other parts have been in use since the early days of the Church. Some prayers were composed during the Middle Ages and the Reformation, while others are the product of the Church in the present day. The prayer book connects us with the past, and at the same time answers our needs in the modern world. It is the heritage given us by the leading of the Holy Spirit working through countless Christians, some of them spiritual giants, and some of them ordinary men and women like ourselves, but all in need of Christ. The first Book of Common Prayer of the Church of England was published in 1549 (BCP, pp. 866-867), and all subsequent Anglican prayer books, with whatever changes, and in whatever languages, bear the stamp and the tradition of that book, which itself carries on the tradition of the ancient Church.

171. **Q.** May we use the prayer book in our family and private prayers, as well as in our corporate prayers and worship?
A. The Book of Common Prayer can be a great help in our family and private prayers. Although we should not feel bound to it, and should use our own free prayers and words as well as other books as helps to our devotions,

the prayer book offers a variety of different kinds of prayer and broadens our prayer experience, while offering valuable guidance in the faith. It also contains special devotions for family or individual use (BCP, pp. 136-140), and a great treasure of prayers and thanksgivings for all occasions (pp. 809-841, etc.).

172. **Q.** What is the Church Year?
A. The Church Year is the yearly recalling of the great acts of God, especially in Jesus Christ. In Israel, the Passover, commemorating God's liberation of the people of Israel from slavery in Egypt, was the central festival of the year. From the first years of the Christian Church, Easter, the commemoration of Christ's resurrection and our redemption, was celebrated with "paschal joy." Later, other days and seasons were gradually added. Advent, Christmas, Epiphany, Lent, Holy Week, Good Friday, the Easter Season, Ascension, and Pentecost. In this way we recall the drama of the life of Christ and of God's work of salvation and sanctification in an orderly sequence. By following the Church Year with the seasons, we are reminded of the whole Christian faith, rather than concentrating on just a part of it. The prayer book appoints proper prayers (the Collects) and passages of scripture (the Lessons, Epistles, and Gospels) to be read each day in accordance with the calendar. We also commemorate through "saints' days" many of the holy people of Christian history who have left us examples for our lives.

173. **Q.** What is the Hymnal?
A. The Hymnal is a collection of songs and chants of praise, thanksgiving, penitence, and prayer. It gathers together the outpourings of the hearts of people in many lands and ages, and through their words and melodies we express ourselves to God. When the whole congregation joins hearts and voices together in singing and making "a joyful noise to the Lord," it is a wonderful way to

praise God. The hymns are also a treasure of prayer and often express the faith in simple ways which speak to the heart (Psalms 81:1-3; 95:1-2; 100:1; Eph. 5:19; Col. 3:16). The Hymnals of the Episcopal Church of 1940 and 1982 are the authorized books to be used in our services and provide settings for parts of the liturgy and hymns to be sung each Sunday and on other occasions.

174. **Q.** Why do the clergy of the Episcopal Church wear special vestments?

A. When the clergy or the laity lead services in the Church, they are not doing it as individuals, but as representatives of the people to help them express their praises and prayers to God. The clergy are also acting as God's representatives to the people to declare God's Word and God's forgiveness. Vestments symbolize the Church's authority to do this. They also connect us with past ages and remind us that the Church and its services are not just temporary things, but partake of the eternal. Vestments have been used since the time of Aaron in the Old Testament (Ex. 28). Different churches and different traditions may use slightly different vestments, but all are worn, not to glorify the individual, but to the glory of God and for the beauty and order of our corporate worship.

175. **Q.** What are the Church colors?

A. The Church colors are used in many traditions for vestments and hangings in the Church. They vary with the Church Year, of which they are reminders, and add beauty to our worship, in keeping with the holiness of God (Ex. 28:4-6; 35:25; 36:8; Psalm 27:4; Rev. 4:1-5). In some churches, where simplicity is stressed, the church colors are not used, and certainly they are not essential or required for worship, nor is there an "official" color scheme. The most common usage is: *white* for seasons and events of joy—Christmas, Epiphany, and Easter; *purple* for seasons of penitence—Advent and Lent; *red* for the Holy

Spirit and for the commemoration of martyrs; and *green* for other times to emphasize Christian growth and hope.

176. **Q.** Why do we kneel, stand, and sit at different times in Church services?

A. We do so to express ourselves more naturally. Worship is not an activity of the mind only, but is entered into with the whole person: body, mind, spirit, and feelings. There are no absolute rules, but we often kneel to pray and confess our sins as an expression of our relationship to Almighty God (1 Kngs. 8:54; Psalm 95:6; Acts 20:36; Rom. 14:11). We usually sit to hear God's Word, for that is the most comfortable way to prepare our hearts and minds to listen. And we stand to raise our voices in praise, to declare our faith, and to hear the Gospel proclaimed.

177. **Q.** Why do some people make the sign of the cross over themselves, bow, genuflect (kneel momentarily on one knee), or do other ceremonial acts during the worship services?

A. All of these "manual acts" are done to honor God in Christ. They are forms of prayer, just as much as words are. They remind us that service to God is something we do, not just think about. Manual acts just as our spoken prayers should never be used to disrupt the worship of others or be forced upon others in the congregation.

178. **Q.** Is the church building a special place?

A. Yes. It is a holy place set apart as sacred to God for the purpose of worship and prayer (1 Kngs. 8:27-30; Mk. 11:17). Though the building itself may be very simple, it is holy because it is dedicated to God, and we treat it and the things that are in it with reverence.

179. **Q.** What are some of the things we find in Episcopal church buildings?

A. The altar or holy table is in the most prominent

position in Episcopal churches. There, the Holy Eucharist is celebrated. There may also be a pulpit from which sermons are preached and a lectern from which the Bible is read. In many churches there is a font near the entrance for the initiating sacrament of Baptism. There are many other things which assist us in our worship and enhance the beauty of the liturgy. All are to be used for the glory of God.

Questions to Think About—VI

a. How can we prevent written prayers from becoming mere dry formalisms, without life?
b. Some people say they can pray better in "the great outdoors," or in their homes, rather than in church. What do you think?
c. Some people say that it is very selfish to pray for ourselves, because God has a lot of other people to care for, and the laws of nature are not going to be changed just for us. Furthermore, God knows what we want before we pray, so it is presumptuous to make these petitions. Is this true?

VII The Sacraments

180. **Q.** What special means of receiving grace has God given us, through Christ and the Church?
A. God has given us the *sacraments*.

181. **Q.** What are the sacraments?
A. The sacraments are outward and visible signs of inward and spiritual grace, given by Christ as sure and certain means by which we receive that grace (BCP, p. 857). We use many things to signify an inner meaning, such as flags, paper money, words, or shaking hands. A sacrament is such an act or sign, given us by Christ or ordained by the Church according to the guidance of the Holy Spirit. We can receive God's grace in other ways, but since the sacraments are ordained by God, they are a pledge and an assurance that through them we may receive God's grace.

182. **Q.** What are the two great sacraments of the Gospel?
A. The two great sacraments given by Christ to his Church are Holy Baptism and the Holy Eucharist (BCP, p. 858).

183. **Q.** What other sacramental rites evolved in the Church under the guidance of the Holy Spirit?
A. Other sacramental rites which evolved in the Church include confirmation, ordination, holy matrimony, reconciliation of a penitent, and unction (BCP, p. 860).

184. **Q.** How do they differ from the two sacraments of the Gospel?
A. Although they are means of grace, they are not necessary for all persons in the same way that Baptism and the Eucharist are (BCP, p. 860).

185. **Q.** What is Holy Baptism?
A. Holy Baptism is the sacrament by which God adopts us as his children and makes us members of Christ's Body, the Church, and inheritors of the kingdom of God (BCP, p. 858).

186. **Q.** Are not all people children of God?
A. All people are created by God and called to be God's children, but because of our sin and separation from God, this relationship is effectively obscured. In Holy Baptism this relationship is restored by God's grace, through a new spiritual birth.

187. **Q.** What is the outward and visible sign in Baptism?
A. The outward and visible sign in Baptism is water, in which the person is baptized in the Name of the Father, and of the Son, and of the Holy Spirit (BCP, p. 858).

188. **Q.** Why did Christ command water to be used?
A. Christ commanded water to be used because it is the universal means of washing, and Baptism signifies the washing away of our sins through Christ's Atonement. Also, as we read in Romans 6:3-4, Baptism (which once was by immersion) symbolizes the death and burial of our old self of sin (going down under the water), and the rising again to new life of the child of God. Through Baptism we participate sacramentally in the death and resurrection of Jesus. Just as Christ was crucified and buried, and then rose again, so we, through him, may die to sin, and be born again to eternal life (Jn. 3:5; Col. 2:12; 1 Pet. 2:24).

189. **Q.** What is the inward and spiritual grace in Baptism?
A. The inward and spiritual grace in Baptism is union with Christ in his death and resurrection, birth into God's family the Church, forgiveness of sins, and new life in the Holy Spirit (BCP, p. 858).

190. **Q.** Does this mean that after Baptism we will sin no more?
A. No. As long as we are in this world, we will be subject to sin and self-centeredness, but through Baptism we are consciously placed in a new covenant relationship to God, and through prayer and our life in the Church, we can receive new strength from the Holy Spirit to enable us to overcome sin and grow more and more in God's love.

191. **Q.** What is required of us at Baptism?
A. It is required that we renounce Satan, repent of our sins, and accept Jesus as our Lord and Savior (BCP, p. 858). When we accept Jesus as our Lord and Savior, it means that we put our whole trust in his grace and love (Lk. 15:18-19; Acts 2:36-39; Rom. 4:20-22; Heb. 10:22-23; BCP, p. 302).

192. **Q.** Why then are infants baptized, even though they cannot fulfill these requirements?
A. Infants are baptized so that they can share in the new life in Christ as members of his Church which he created through the New Covenant.

193. **Q.** How are the promises for infants made and carried out?
A. Promises are made for them by their parents and sponsors, who guarantee that the infants will be brought up within the Church, to know Christ and be able to follow him (BCP, p. 858-59). In the sacrament of Baptism, God's grace is the most important thing, not our imperfect repentance and weak faith. The Holy Spirit can work in ways we do not know, even in infants who have no understanding (Jn. 3:8; Rom. 8:26-27).

194. **Q.** What are the responsibilities of parents and sponsors?
A. Parents and sponsors (or godparents) are responsible for seeing that these children are brought up in the Christian faith and life. They promise to help them, by their

prayers and witness to grow into the full stature of Christ (BCP, p. 302). Parents and godparents should pray for their godchildren every day, and especially remember them on their birthdays and baptismal anniversaries. Wherever possible they should see that they continue to go to church school and church, and when the time comes are prepared for Confirmation. They should help them spiritually and in other ways when help is needed.

195. **Q.** What promises are made at Baptism?
A. At Baptism we promise to *renounce* the spirit of evil, and all self-centered pride and ambition which keeps us from the love of God and our fellow human beings. We promise to *believe* in Jesus Christ as our Lord and Savior, and all other articles of the Apostle's Creed. And we promise to *follow* Christ and obey him in all we do, to continue in his fellowship, to witness to him, to love and serve our neighbors, and to strive for justice and peace (BCP, p. 302-305).

196. **Q.** Why is each candidate presented by name in Baptism (BCP, p. 307)?
A. The use of our names reminds us that God loves and cares for each individual person as one of God's children (Jn. 10:3).

197. **Q.** Who is authorized to baptize?
A. Any baptized person is permitted to baptize, and in the Episcopal Church we recognize baptisms of whatever denomination, if they are performed with water in the Name of the Father, of the Son, and of the Holy Spirit. In an emergency it may be the duty of baptized laypeople to baptize according to the form on p. 313 of the prayer book and to inform the priest of an appropriate parish later on.

198. **Q.** Does being baptized mean we will automatically be saved?

A. No. Baptism is ordinarily required as the first step on the way to salvation, placing ourselves in God's hands in a saving relationship of love. If we are to receive the promises of God, then we must keep our side of the covenant by faith and following Christ in his way of love (1 Cor. 10:1-15).

199. **Q.** Is it impossible for an unbaptized person to be saved?
A. No. With God all things are possible (Mk. 10:27), but since Christ has ordained this sacrament for us as a means of receiving God's grace, to refuse it willingly is to our peril (Jn. 3:5, see Q. 177).

200. **Q.** What additional help in the life of faith does the Church give us?
A. Confirmation, or the Laying on of Hands.

201. **Q.** What is Confirmation?
A. Confirmation is the rite in which we express a mature commitment to Christ, and receive strength from the Holy Spirit through prayer and the laying on of hands by a bishop (BCP, p. 860). It is a voluntary reaffirmation (or confirmation) of the promises made in Baptism to renounce sin, believe in God, and follow God's commandments, and to acccept Jesus Christ as our Lord and Savior. It is also a strengthening (or confirming) in grace by the Holy Spirit to live and grow in the Christian life of love. For those who received infant Baptism, Confirmation means the free and conscious taking on of the promises made for us by our parents and godparents at Baptism, after study of the Christian faith and way. For those receiving adult Baptism, Confirmation complements it, and should be performed at the same time, as it was in the Early Church (BCP, p. 309).

202. **Q.** Who first administered Confirmation?
A. The apostles first administered Confirmation (Acts

8:14-17). Of course it was not "Confirmation" then, but it became so in the history of the Church.

203. **Q.** By whom is Confirmation administered now?
A. Confirmation is administered now by bishops, who are the successors to the apostles. Through the bishops, by the power of the Holy Spirit, all who receive Confirmation are sacramentally united with the apostles, the Universal Church, and with Jesus Christ. Since at Confirmation we acknowledge our responsibility to contribute to the Church's life, we should study the faith with prayer, so that we can live by this faith and be able to communicate it to others. It is both appropriate and pastorally desirable that the affirmations should be received by a bishop as representing the diocese and the worldwide Church; and that the bishop should recall the applicants to their Christian mission, and, by a laying on of hands, transmit his blessing, with a prayer for the strenghthening graces. This occasion is a significant and unrepeatable event; thus the prayer book provides alternative forms for the *reception* of persons into the Episcopal Church who have already been confirmed by bishops in other communions that have retained apostolic succession, and for the *reaffirmation* of their Confirmation intentions by those who have fallen away from the faith (see BCP, pp. 309, 418-19).

204. **Q.** Are we made members of the Church by Confirmation?
A. No. We are already made members at Baptism. Confirmation renews us in our membership as communicants, privileged to receive the special means of grace which Christ has provided for us to help us to continue in his way.

205. **Q.** What sacrament did Christ give us to bring us into union with him and with each other, and to strenghten us in our life of faith and love?
A. Christ gave us the Holy Eucharist.

206. **Q.** What is the Holy Eucharist?
A. The Holy Eucharist is the sacrament commanded by Christ for the continual remembrance of his life, death, and resurrection, until his coming again (BCP, p. 859).

207. **Q.** Why is the Eucharist called a sacrifice?
A. Because the Eucharist, the Church's sacrifice of praise and thanksgiving, is the way by which the sacrifice of Christ is made present, and in which he unites us to his one offering of himself (BCP, p. 859). In Old Testament times the people of Israel sacrificed animals to God, trying to offer the best they had, and believing that somehow the blood of the slain animal, poured over the altar and sprinkled on the people, could unite them with God in a covenant relationship and bring about forgiveness of sins (Ex. 24:6-8). But already in the Old Testament, the prophets taught that this slaughter of dumb animals could not, of itself, bring about its purpose (Isa. 1:11; Mic. 6:6-8; Psalms 50:7-15; 51:16-17). Christ's death on the cross did what the Old Testament sacrifices could never do. Christ offered himself to God completely, once for all, a perfect life and a voluntary and sinless death for the sins of the whole world. We still need to give ourselves to God, but because of our self-centeredness, we can never give our whole life, and our self-offering is very incomplete and imperfect. Christ promised us that, by faith in him, we can identify our imperfect offering of ourselves with his one perfect sacrifice, and so enter into the New Covenant of grace (Jn. 3:16; 6:54; 12:32).

208. **Q.** By what other names is the Holy Eucharist known?
A. The Holy Eucharist is called the Lord's Supper or Holy Communion; it is also known as the Divine Liturgy, the Mass, and the Great Offering (BCP, p. 859).

209. **Q.** What is the outward and visible sign in the Eucharist?
A. The outward and visible sign in the Eucharist is bread

and wine, given and received according to God's command (BCP, p. 859).

210. **Q.** What is the inward and spiritual grace given in the Eucharist?
A. The inward and spiritual grace given in the Holy Eucharist is the Body and Blood of Christ given to his people and received by faith (BCP, p. 859).

211. **Q.** When and how was the Holy Eucharist instituted?
A. The Holy Eucharist was instituted by Christ at the Last Supper. On the night before he died on the cross, Jesus, preparing for Passover with his disciples, took bread, gave thanks, broke it, and gave it to them saying, "Take, eat, this is my body which is given for you. Do this in remembrance of me." And after supper he took the cup, and when he had given thanks, he gave it to them saying, "Drink of it all of you; for this is my blood of the new covenant, which is poured out for many for the forgiveness of sins. Do this, as often as you drink it, in remembrance of me" (1 Cor. 11:23-26; Mt. 26:26-29; Mk. 14:22-25; Lk. 22:19-20).

212. **Q.** What did Christ mean by these words and actions?
A. Christ meant to give us a memorial of himself and his atonement by which we might, through recalling his death and resurrection, experience his presence in our midst, and be joined with him in spiritual union now in this world, as a pledge of the perfect union in the world to come. We do not know specifically how this happens, but we believe it to be so, and for over 1900 years, even in the midst of persecutions, Christians have found it to be true.

213. **Q.** What did Christ mean by saying, "This is my blood of the New Covenant"?
A. Our Lord was referring to his own sacrificial death for the forgiveness of our sins, by which God made a New

Covenant with us through Jesus Christ, so that we, by faith in Jesus Christ, might have communion with the Divine, and overcome our enemies of sin and death. The consecrated bread and wine thus become for us the effective signs of the New Covenant.

214. **Q.** What are the benefits we receive in the Lord's Supper?
A. The benefits we receive are the forgiveness of our sins, the strengthening of our union with Christ and one another, and the foretaste of the heavenly banquet which is our nourishment in eternal life (BCP, p. 859-60). As our bodies are strengthened by the bread and wine, so our souls are refreshed and strengthened by the Body and Blood of Christ. Through the Lord's Supper we are united with Christ and are made one with all those who partake of the same sacrament. This unity, or *communion*, with Christ and with others breaks down the barriers which sin has caused to separate us, and brings to us all the love and grace of Christ to fill our lives and change them. For this reason we call the Eucharist "the Holy Communion" (1 Cor. 10:16-17). It is a window looking into eternity and foreshadows the heavenly banquet when we shall be with Christ in his kingdom. Christ, the great high priest, celebrates the feast, and gives us himself in the sacrament, a foretaste and earnest of the heavenly communion. It is the eternal breaking into the present (Mt. 26:29; 1 Cor. 11:26; Heb. 9:11-15).

215. **Q.** What is required of us when we come to the Eucharist?
A. We should have faith in Christ, his atoning death and victorious resurrection, and in the New Covenant which he established, of which the sacrament of the Lord's Supper is the token and seal. It is also required that we should examine our lives, repent of our sins, and be in love and charity with all people (BCP, p. 860). Perfect repentance, love, and faith are beyond our reach, but we should desire them and direct our wills and our hearts toward them to

come nearer to God. The Holy Eucharist is a means of grace and help to attain this.

216. **Q.** Should we make any special preparations before the Eucharist?
A. Before the Eucharist we should try to prepare ourselves by prayer, thanking God for all the blessings we have received, meditating on God's love, examining ourselves and confessing our sins, trying to make resolutions to amend our lives, bringing them into conformity with Christ. Reading the Bible, the prayer book, or other Christian writings is very helpful. Some Christians practice fasting before Communion and find it a meaningful discipline (Heb. 10:19-25).

217. **Q.** How often should we partake of the Lord's Supper?
A. The Holy Eucharist is "the principal act of Christian worship on the Lord's Day and other major Feasts" (BCP, p. 13), and we should consider it our duty and privilege to participate in that worship if it is at all possible. This has been the custom from the time of the apostles (Acts 20:7).

218. **Q.** What things do we offer to God in the Holy Eucharist?
A. In the Eucharist we offer praise and thanksgiving, bread and wine, and other gifts from our daily lives, of which money is the most common. Praise and thanksgiving include all our prayers, our hymns and anthems, the reading of the Word, the beauty of music and flowers and liturgy, and our joy in the Lord (BCP, pp. 335,363). Bread and wine symbolize our life and work and God's creation. In the Early Church, believers often offered bread and wine which they had made themselves. These in a very real sense represented their life and work. It is significant that Christ chose these material things made with human labor, using God's gifts of creation, the wheat and the grape, and not purely natural foods like milk and

honey. Furthermore, they were the common food of the day, not luxuries or mysterious exotic things. Today, parishioners usually have not made the bread and the wine themselves, but we offer our money which, in many ways, is a real offering of our work and lives. Money can be used for the wrong reasons, as can also our lives and labor, but there is nothing wrong with it in itself, and it can be used for great good. "Where your treasure is," Jesus said, "there will your heart be also" (Mt. 6:21). Money offered to God is given for holy purposes, and it is an acceptable and necessary offering. Christ takes these imperfect offerings, the symbols of our sinful lives, and incorporates them into his perfect offering of his life, given to God for us on the cross. Christ then gives us back our offerings, the bread and the wine, changed into his Body and Blood, the symbols of his perfect life. We give our sinful lives, and we receive God's eternal life. By partaking of Christ's gift of new life, we are renewed and strengthened to do God's will in love.

219. **Q.** Is the Holy Eucharist only a memorial of something that happened in the past?
A. No. The Holy Eucharist is also a *present* realization and concrete experience of Christ's living presence and continual giving of himself to us, and it looks forward to the *future* perfect communion with Christ in heaven.

220. **Q.** How should we receive the Body and Blood of Christ?
A. We should receive these gifts reverently, praying silently, offering ourselves up to God, asking to be made one with Christ and to be used by him in showing his love to all people. Most Anglicans receive the consecrated bread on the palm of one hand which is placed over the upturned palm of the other, and put the sacrament directly into the mouth without taking it up in the fingers. When receiving from the chalice, it is best to guide it by taking it lightly at the base with one hand, while the priest

holds it, and to lift one's face slightly so that the priest can see whether one has received or not. After receiving, we should return to our place and pray silently, thanking God for this great privilege, and asking that the grace which we have received may be manifested in a better life of love to God and our neighbors.

221. **Q.** Who may receive the Holy Eucharist?
A. Only those who have been baptized may receive the Holy Communion. We must also examine our lives, repent of our sins, and be in love and charity with all people. In addition we are required to have faith in Christ's atonement and to believe that he is present in this sacrament. An Exhortation on pages 316-17 of the prayer book is a very clear guide for this purpose. Communicants of other denominations who fulfill these requirements are also welcome when visiting to receive the Eucharist at Episcopal churches. The sacrament should never be received casually or as a matter of course. It should be remembered that the Holy Eucharist is "The Liturgy for the Proclamation of the Word of God and Celebration of the Holy Communion" (BCP, p. 315). Those who come to the service late, after the Gospel, should seriously consider whether they should receive or not, and normally no one who comes after the Confession should receive. Only if we make sincere preparations of repentence, love, and faith can we receive the great blessings which Christ offers to us in this sacrament.

222. **Q.** Can those who are unable to attend church services also participate?
A. Yes. Even though people are unable to attend church services because of sickness or some other reason, they may join spiritually in their prayers and praises. By reading the services in the prayer book and the Bible we can experience spiritual communion with others who are also worshiping God. The prayer book also provides special

services for the sick and for the administration of the sacraments in a special Eucharist (BCP, pp. 396-99, 453-61).

223. **Q.** In what ways does the Holy Eucharist express the corporate nature of Christian life in the church and the world?
A. The Holy Eucharist is of tremendous help for our individual lives in the faith, but it should never be thought of only as that. In the Holy Eucharist we meet together as the family of God, and through our corporate participation in the liturgy we offer up our lives together and receive Christ's blessings as a fellowship. In the giving of the peace we assert our unity with each other in Christ, and this is confirmed when we all partake of the one bread, receiving the One Body of Christ so that we may *be* the Body of Christ. At the end of the service we are sent "forth into the world. . .to love and serve the Lord" and to show Christ's love and the truth of the gospel to all people. The Holy Eucharist is not a private retreat from the world, but a corporate participation in which we bring the concerns of the world before God and go forth to minister God's healing grace to the world's needs.

Questions to Think About—VII

a. Could a person be a Christian without receiving any sacraments?
b. What reasons could you give for infant Baptism, or for believer's (adult) Baptism?
c. If Christ is always present with us, in what way is he especially present in the Holy Eucharist?

VIII   Christian Life

224. **Q.** Is the proclamation of the gospel to those outside the Church the responsibility of only specially trained persons—the ordained clergy?

A. No. All of us are commissioned by Christ to tell others by word and deed of God's mercy and love, and to try to bring them into God's family, the Church, so that they too may experience that love (Mt. 28:19). This is not only a responsibility given us by Christ, but a privilege which we should be glad to carry out in thanksgiving and love. Since we ourselves have come to know God and to hold the Christian faith through others, we can show our thanks by being the means through which others may come to know God and believe. If we love our neighbors, as Christ commands us, we cannot help but share this most precious gift with them.

225. **Q.** What do we call this proclamation of the gospel, and how is it done?

A. It is called evangelism, telling the good news, and it is done by word and by the witness of our lives. We should tell others what we have learned and experienced and what God has done for us through Christ. Reading Christian books, pamphlets, and periodicals may help us to express this in words, and we can introduce these writings, as well as the Bible and Book of Common Prayer, to those outside the Church. The witness of our lives is equally important. If we show God's love and Christian joy in our lives, others will see, and this will help us to lead them to Christ and his Church (Mt. 5:16). It is true that because we have different gifts, some can lead others more easily, but all of us can do something, bring someone to church, lend a Christian book or magazine, say a word, or make a witness in our lives. Evangelism is the responsibility of all Christians, not just of the clergy.

226. **Q.** Is this responsibility for evangelism and witness only to those living in our own community?

A. No. Christ commanded us to be witnesses "to the end of the earth" (Acts 1:8), and we share this responsibility for witness with Christians all over the world. Not only can we support the mission of our church overseas where our representatives are working together with Christians of the "younger churches" for the spread of the gospel, but we can also welcome the assistance of those from other countries to work with us in our own communities among those who have never really heard the gospel in a way they could understand or accept. By sharing the gifts and insights which God has given us in our different situations we can more completely present Christ to the world and bring the prophetic power of the gospel's love and justice to bear on the social and economic institutions of our country as well as other nations.

227. **Q.** Shouldn't we try to make our own country perfectly Christian before sending missionaries abroad?

A. No. If the first apostles had waited until Palestine had become perfectly Christian, Christianity would never have spread to other countries at all, and we ourselves would not be Christians. Our faith is the heritage of countless others who have gone before us, and we must continue their work.

228. **Q.** Is it right to try to impose our faith on those who already have faith in some other religion?

A. We should always respect the beliefs of others and share and work with them in any way we can. Evangelism does not mean using force or undue pressure on people to abandon their previous faith. Evangelism is sharing in thanksgiving and love the message of God's love for us in Christ with those who are open to hear it. It is not within our power to make people believe, for conversion is the work of the Holy Spirit.

229. **Q.** Who are the ministers of the Church?
A. The ministers of the Church are lay persons, bishops, priests, and deacons (BCP, p. 855).

230. **Q.** What is the ministry of the laity?
A. The ministry of lay persons is to represent Christ and his Church; to bear witness to him wherever they may be; and, according to the gifts given to them, to carry on Christ's work of reconciliation in the world; and to take their place in the life, worship, and governance of the Church (BCP, p. 855).

231. **Q.** Can we witness to Christ in our work?
A. Yes. Our work can be an offering to God and our neighbors and an expression of love for others, if it is done well. Through our actions and our words we may also be able to influence those with whom we work and, if possible, bring them to faith in Christ.

232. **Q.** Is it important what kind of work we do?
A. Yes. God has given us different gifts and talents, and every person has a vocation to serve (or minister) through work in some special way. Christians should think of themselves as representatives of Christ's Church in the world, and they should think seriously about what God has called them to do in this life. Sometimes the Holy Spirit gives us a clear calling to a particular kind of work, such as medicine, teaching, engineering, science, law, or the ordained ministry. Sometimes we may not be aware of any clear guidance or vocation from God, yet God may be leading us to our lives' work through various circumstances and our own interests and aptitudes. What is most important is to be able to do our work as an offering to God and as an expression of love to others. Even though it sometimes seems unimportant and uninteresting, all honest work is important for ourselves, our families, and society. This is true of study, which is preparatory work.

It is true of housekeeping and the raising of children, which are among the most important kinds of work and ways of showing our love for others, and which should not be left for one member of the family to do alone. Even those who, because of health or age, are not able to do physical work, can serve in expressing love in human relationships and in the work of prayer.

233. **Q.** Does the value of our lives depend only on the work we do?

A. No. All of life is not work. Recreation, play, building friendships, culture, the arts, and just relaxation and sleep have their place in God's plan for us. Like worship and rest, they are a re-creation, a gathering of forces or preparation which enables us to realize our full humanity and selfhood within the context of loving human relationships, in order that we may better express ourselves in love to others.

234. **Q.** How can we take our "place in the life, worship, and governance of the Church" (BCP, p. 855)?

A. The Church is the family of God, the fellowship of love, and as we should share our joys and sorrows together, so we should join together in that high service which is the essence of our being, to glorify and thank God who is our creator, redeemer, preserver, and the giver of all good things. In our worship we come together to hear God's word and the teaching of the Church—not just our own private and sometimes mistaken opinions of what God's will is for us. In our worship we confess our sins, join in prayer, and receive the grace of the sacraments. Through these we are not only strengthened individually, but the Church as a corporate body also is empowered to serve in the world to meet the problems of society and to be a redeeming force for the needs of people. It is our duty and privilege "to come together week by week for corporate worship," and we should also bring others with us.

235. **Q.** What sort of ways are there in which we can serve in the Church?

A. There are many things which the laity can do in the Church to serve, besides joining in the corporate worship. We can serve in various groups or committees, help with the Church school, youth groups, or other organizations. Many people help in cleaning the church, giving flowers, singing in the choir, acting as ushers, or visiting the sick or lapsed members. There are full-time jobs for some in the areas of Christian education, social work, music, and other forms of service connected with the Church. As members of the Church we may also join in the Church's corporate efforts of relief for the poor and oppressed and for the reform of evils in our society. All of us should try to use our time and talents for the Church in some way, but we should also realize that we are witnesses and workers for God in the world, and that this is perhaps the most important aspect of the ministry of the laity.

236. **Q.** What is ordination?

A. Ordination is the rite in which God, through the Church, gives authority and the grace of the Holy Spirit to those being made bishops, priests, and deacons, through prayer and the laying on of hands by bishops (BCP, pp. 860-61). All people should consider prayerfully whether God calls them to the ordained ministry, and parents should help their children by presenting this and other vocations as possibilities to them. At the same time, the Church must test and train those who feel called, and only those who are qualified and needed can be ordained for service in the Church. (For the nature of the ministry of bishops, priests, and deacons, see BCP, pp. 855 and 856.)

237. **Q.** What is the duty of all Christians?

A. The duty of all Christians is to follow Christ, to come together week by week for corporate worship, and to work, pray, and give for the spread of the kingdom of God (BCP, p. 856).

238. **Q.** Why is it important to give a part of our money to the Church?

A. In modern society, money is an important and necessary part of our lives, and to give it to the Church can be one of the best ways to give a part of ourselves to God. Of course, it costs money to build and maintain a church, and the congregation has the responsibility of supporting the clergy and all the parish's work for its members and the world. In addition we should support the diocesan and national church and the mission and social services of the Church both at home and abroad. Our giving should not be thought of merely as meeting a budget to support the program of a church, but rather as a token of our thanksgiving and self-offering to God.

239. **Q.** How much money should we give to God through the Church?

A. We should give as much as we can. There is no rule or law about exactly how much to give to the Church, since Christian giving should be based on a free decision showing our faith and thanksgiving. In general we can say that those who have more should give more (Tobit 4:7-11, 2 Cor. 9:6-7). Christ taught that the sacrificial gift of the poor was of much more value than the gift from the surplus riches of the wealthy (Lk. 21:1-4).

240. **Q.** What is tithing?

A. Tithing is the ancient practice of giving a tenth of all we have to God. From Old Testament times (Gen. 28:22), and in the early Christian Church there has been the custom of giving one tenth of one's income to God. The Episcopal Church has endorsed tithing as the standard for Christian giving. This should not be a rigid, mechanically interpreted rule. Some can afford more, and for some it might actually be too much. Since the amount we should give is often a very difficult decision to make, the tithe is a useful guide, and by adopting it we usually find we are gladly giving more than formerly. We all have the responsibility of deciding, after serious thought and prayer, how much we can give as a thank-offering each week, month, or year, out of all that God has given us. Our decision should be based not merely on what the parish needs for its budget, nor on what other people are likely to give, but on what we ourselves can and should give to God. When we think of all that God has given us, and especially of Jesus giving his life for us, we realize how small a token our giving is (2 Cor. 8:1-5, 9). Some parishes also practice a kind of tithing when they are raising money for a building or some other project, by giving one tenth of the money for the mission of the Church, and some parishes aim to give at least half of their yearly budget for purposes outside the parish.

241. **Q.** Should all our giving be to the Church, or should we also support various other causes and agencies?

A. Besides our giving to the Church for local, diocesan, national, and mission needs, we should also give to help victims of poverty, neglect, natural disasters, or social injustice, and where possible work to correct these evils. As St. John writes, "If any one has the world's goods and sees his brother in need, yet closes his heart against him, how does God's love abide in him?" (1 Jn. 3:17). Christians should not only help those whom they see have need, but should actively seek out and find places where their help is needed. In the Early Church and middle ages, almost all charitable work was done by the Church. Now there are many agencies outside as well as in the Church, together with the government, which carry on the work of care and love, and we should certainly support them too. Christ's words in Matthew 25:40 should always be remembered: "As you did it to one of the least of these my brethren, you did it to me." We may consider our giving within and outside the Church as equally gifts to God, who gives to all equally (Mt. 5:45), and decide, after prayer, how much we should give to each.

242. **Q.** What place do beauty and the arts have in Christian life?

A. We believe in God who is absolute beauty, goodness, and holiness, who has given us the gift of perceiving beauty and of sharing in the creation of it (Gen. 1:31; Psalm 27:4). In art we seek to create and express a part of that beauty and truth which God has given us, and to help others to see it. The great artists, musicians, and writers are those who have reached a higher and more intense level of perception of God's beauty and truth, and by expressing them in art, have helped us to see, even if more dimly, a part of their vision. God, who is love, created a world of beauty, and wills us not to desecrate that beauty with pollution and a dreary and ugly "culture." Rather, we are to work with God in love to make life richer, better, and more beautiful, within the natural beauty of the earth, the sea, the sky, and all living things. Beauty and the arts are essential to the wholeness of society and true humanity. In all this we look forward to better things, to the vision of the absolute beauty which God is preparing for us in the eternal city. Beauty is eternal, and all that is beautiful will endure, transfigured and redeemed in the kingdom of heaven (Mk. 14:3-9; Prov. 8:22-31; Rev. 21:1-7, 22-27).

243. **Q.** Is the search for truth a part of God's will for us?

A. Yes. God is absolute truth and has given us reason and intelligence, so that we, alone in this earthly creation, can know and understand ourselves, the world, and even, in part, God. Thinkers, scholars, explorers, and scientists have been searching to discover the truths of God's world, and to help all of us to know them too. Knowledge and

91

love of the truth are of the essence of humanity. To seek the truth is, in part, to seek God. Our use of knowledge must always be in the context of love, for love is the highest truth. Here on earth we see dimly, but in heaven we shall see the full truth in the glorious light of God's love (Job 28; Prov. 8; Jn. 8:31-32; 14:6; 1 Cor. 13:8-13; 2 Cor. 4:6-7; 1 Tim. 2:3-4).

244. **Q.** What is Holy Matrimony?
A. Holy Matrimony is Christian marriage, in which a woman and man enter into a life-long union, make their vows before God and the Church, and receive the grace and blessing of God to help them fulfill their vows (BCP, p. 861).

245. **Q.** If we think of the Church as our spiritual family, is the human family just a physical and social convenience?
A. No. The family is an institution ordained by God and serves a sacred purpose. God has blessed marriage as a means of mutual fulfillment and help, both physical and spiritual (Gen. 2:18, 24), and as a holy bond of love for the bringing forth and nurture of children. The home is meant to be a place of love, and the family is the agent entrusted with the mission of bringing up children in health, love, and Christian faith.

246. **Q.** Why should the marriage service normally be performed in the Church?
A. Marriages should normally be celebrated in the Church because marriage is a sacramental rite, a sacred bond, and should be blessed within the congregation of the faithful. Vows which are made in the house of God, before the altar, have a solemnity difficult to find elsewhere. The prayers, witness, and promise of the congregation testify that this is an act in which the whole family of the Church is deeply concerned (BCP, p. 425). It is right to start this life-long union in God's Church where we experience sacramentally God's perfect love.

247. **Q.** Is it necessary to confer with the minister before a marriage?

A. Yes. Since marriage is of such great importance to all concerned, the couple should confer well in advance with their minister, the priest of the church in which they will be married.

248. **Q.** What does the Declaration of Intention in Canon 17 say of marriage?

A. The Declaration of Intention says that marriage is "a lifelong union of husband and wife, for the purpose of mutual fellowship, encouragement, and understanding, for the procreation (if it may be) of children, and their physical and spiritual nurture, for the safeguarding and benefit of society."

249. **Q.** Who are the ministers at a wedding?

A. The man and the woman are the true ministers. The ordained minister represents God's Church to them, and with the prayers of the congregation, gives them the Church's blessing. It is the man and the woman who make the vows which constitute the marriage, and it is they who join hands and exchange the rings, the sacramental, outward signs of the marriage.

250. **Q.** Does the Church recognize civil marriages, or those made outside the Church?

A. Yes. Since it is the man and woman who perform the marriage and not the priest, the Church recognizes civil marriages, and a form for "The Blessing of a Civil Marriage" is provided in the prayer book (p. 433).

251. **Q.** Why does the priest usually take the hands of the couple and join them together?

A. This symbolizes that they give themselves to God and receive their partners as though from God. In the same way the rings are given to the priest who blesses them before the couple exchange them, signifying that they and all they have are blessed and bound together by God in love and peace.

252. **Q.** What significance do the rings have?
A. Rings are sacramental tokens of vows of marriage, together with the joining of hands. A ring is a circle, symbolizing perfection and the eternal nature of the marriage vows. The precious metal used for the rings signifies the sacredness of marriage, and they are placed on the fingers least used, partly to remind us of the purity of married love. By giving them to each other, a couple promise to give themselves and all they have to each other for life (BCP, p. 427).

253. **Q.** What practical considerations should be kept in mind when planning a Christian wedding?
A. Beauty and stateliness are well and fitting, but extremes of costly and lavish display should be avoided. Although unobtrusive photography may be permitted, the priest's permission must be obtained. The music in the marriage ceremony should be appropriate to the Christian meaning of the service. In the church the simplicity, beauty, and deep meaning of the service should never be obscured by the introduction of, and fussiness about, meaningless details, and although hospitality may require a reception for guests, there is no reason to make this an affair that attempts to impress others. Ostentation and extravagance have no place in a true Christian wedding.

254. **Q.** Is marriage performed at any time of the year?
A. It is the custom of the Church not to have weddings in Advent or Lent or on Sundays, although exceptions might be made for sufficient reasons. In any event, the minister should always be consulted *before* making a final decision on the date.

255. **Q.** Is the procreation of children a duty of those who marry?

A. In normal circumstances Christians who marry should desire to have and nurture children. In this way they will be serving and working with God, who created us, and gave us the gift of life and the joy of sharing in creation. Bringing children up in the Christian faith advances the cause of Christ. Of course, there may be special circumstances which make it impossible or inadvisable to have children, but unless this is so, the decision not to have children is often a selfish one. Some Christian couples decide to adopt a child, and in this way give a Christian home and love to a child who otherwise might not have them. More than a duty, the procreation and nurture of children should be looked on as a privilege and a blessing for which we should thank God (BCP, p. 439-45; Gen. 1:28; Mk. 10:13-16).

256. **Q.** Are Christian parents permitted to plan the number and spacing of their children?

A. Since bringing new life into the world, and the care and nurture of children are of such importance, a man and a woman should not undertake them thoughtlessly, but should decide with prayer and preparation, using their God-given reason. The control of conception (almost always incorrectly called "birth-control"), whether by temporary abstinence or by artificial means (contraceptives), may be practiced by responsible Christian parents in order to ensure their ability to care properly for all their children, and for the promotion of harmony and health in the family and society.

257. **Q.** Should children be baptized soon after their birth?
A. Yes. Through Baptism children are brought into the family of the Church, into the New Covenant relationship to God, made members of Christ, and inheritors of the kingdom of heaven.

258. **Q.** How should parents nurture their children in the Christian faith?

A. Parents should bring their children to Church for Baptism and teach them to pray and read the Bible at home, to lead Christian lives, and to know the Christian faith. This can only be done if the parents themselves do these things and lead their children not only by word but by example.

259. **Q.** How should love be expressed between men and women, or between boys and girls, before marriage?

A. It is impossible to fix rules to define the relationships of friendship, courtship and love. Some people may have only one loyalty for life, which leads to marriage, while others may go through a long series of attachments with varying degrees of seriousness and involvement, pain and joy. Christians should be careful to treat others sincerely, as persons, and not to trifle with their feelings, or use them cynically, as objects for selfish purposes and sensual satisfaction. Sex should not be thought of as just a simple diversion, for it has a profound effect on the total personality, and unless it is directed and controlled, it can be a devastating and enslaving force in our lives.

260. **Q.** Is divorce permissible for Episcopalians?

A. Not ordinarily. Marriage is a life-long union, and in the marriage service the couple vows "to have and to hold...for better for worse, for richer for poorer, in sickness and in health, to love and to cherish, until we are parted by death" (BCP, p. 427). Divorce is not only a breaking of vows, but breaks the all important family bond for any children there may be. Because the Church stresses the sacredness of marriage, a divorced person may not ordinarily remarry in the Church. In exceptional cases, persons whose previous marriage has been dissolved or annulled by a civil court may apply to their bishop for a judgment as to whether they may remarry within the

Church (Canon 18). When such a marriage is permitted, the wedding ceremony should be as simple as possible.

261. **Q.** What is Unction of the Sick?
A. Unction is the rite of anointing the sick with oil, or the laying on of hands, by which God's grace is given for the healing of the spirit, mind, and body (BCP, pp. 861, 455-57).

262. **Q.** What should the Christian's attitude toward sickness be?
A. Sickness is one of the evils of this world to which we are subject. Although it is connected in some way with the sinful condition of all people, we cannot say that a specific sickness is the result of a certain person's sins, unless, of course, there is a direct cause-and-effect connection (Jn. 9:2-3). We should not, therefore, say that God is punishing those who are sick because of their sins (Job). On the contrary, we believe that it is the will of God for all to be well, and that Christ, of his mercy, healed both the bodies and the souls of the sick, and therefore we should use all means, medical and spiritual, to heal them. Doctors, nurses, hospital workers and all who help the sick are doing the work of God; but prayer is equally important, and both the sick people themselves, and others concerned for them, should pray that their sicknesses might be cured (Ecclus. 38:1-14). From ancient times, prayer for the sick, the laying on of hands (Acts 28:8), and anointing have been used (James 5:14-16), and liturgies and prayers are provided in the prayer book (BCP, pp. 453-61). We can also use sicknesses as a means of grace to achieve a closer communion with God and a deeper faith. It may be a time of self-examination, repentance, and prayer. When this is true, sickness becomes a means of blessing, and many have found their true faith in times of sickness or danger. Many saints have been purified and led to new spiritual insights through periods of sickness.

St. Paul testifies that his infirmities were the means of Christ's power being shown to him through his weakness (2 Cor. 12:7-10).

263. **Q.** What is Reconciliation of a Penitent?
A. Reconciliation of a Penitent, or Penance, is the rite in which those who repent of their sins confess them to God in the presence of a priest, and receive the assurance of pardon and the grace of absolution (BCP, pp. 861, 446-52).

264. **Q.** Why is there evil in the world which was created by God?
A. As finite creatures we cannot fully explain why there is evil in the world created by God, who is love (Isa. 45:15). Many evils, such as war, crime, injustice, discrimination, and poverty are directly related to our own sin, and we should work to eliminate these. Other "evils," such as earthquakes, floods, and storms cannot be so explained, and we can only try to reduce the suffering through preventive action and works of mercy to those in distress. For the rest we must accept a certain amount of suffering in this life, and we try to use it positively for our spiritual growth, trusting in God and rising above it, while fighting against that which can be corrected (Deut. 29:29; 2 Cor. 6:4-10). Christ said, "In the world you have tribulation; but be of good cheer, I have overcome the world" (Jn. 16:33).

265. **Q.** What is the Christian hope?
A. The Christian hope is to live with confidence in newness and fullness of life, and to await the coming of Christ in glory, the completion of God's purpose for the world (BCP, p. 861).

266. **Q.** What, then, is our assurance as Christians?
A. Our assurance as Christians is that nothing, even death, shall separate us from the love of God which is in Christ Jesus our Lord (BCP, p. 862; Rom. 8:18, 31-39).

267. **Q.** What should be the Christian's attitude toward death?
A. First, Christians believe that death is not the end, but rather a new beginning, the gateway to a larger life, a new birth in eternity in the presence and love of God. This is not through any inherent immortality we have in ourselves, but is the blessing of God, given through our Savior Jesus Christ. Therefore we do not "grieve as others do who have no hope. For since we believe that Jesus died and rose again, even so, through Jesus, God will bring with him those who have fallen asleep" (1 Thess. 4:13-14). Although there is grief in parting, there should be greater joy in the new and better life, and certainty that fellowship with those who die in the faith is not lost.

Second, Christians should not evade the fact of their own death, nor that it may come at any time. We must, therefore, be prepared for it, knowing that we will live only once on this earth, and that we will be judged by the way we lived this life. "Now is the acceptable time; behold, now is the day of salvation" (2 Cor. 6:2). Now is the time to be reconciled, to forgive, to carry out unkept resolutions, to repent, to make acts of faith, and to show forth works of love.

Third, Christians should, in love, make provision for those whom they will leave when they die. Not to do so often leads to tragic difficulties for bereaved partners, children, parents, or others dependent on them, or those who must act for them after their death. Wills should be made carefully, with legal advice, and consideration should be given for religious and charitable bequests. Such things as joint checking accounts, insurance, and putting one's affairs in order are often of critical importance to those who survive, and they should be attended to as an expression of Christian love.

Life is a gift of God and should be treasured and safeguarded, as well as given and spent, but Christians should have no fear of death and should look on it as God's call to be with Christ in everlasting joy and peace.

268. **Q.** How should Christians mark the death of a member of the household of God?

A. The prayer book provides magnificent services for the Burial of the Dead (BCP, pp. 462-507), full of faith in the Resurrection, of joy and triumph, of assurance and peace, and of great comfort to those who are separated physically from those they love, with all the grief which that involves. Though "we sorrow in sympathy with those who mourn," we should remember that "The liturgy for the dead is an Easter liturgy. It finds all its meaning in the resurrection. Because Jesus was raised from the dead, we, too, shall be raised" (BCP, p. 507). The service should be a corporate one held in the Church, so that the whole fellowship of the family of God may give thanks for a life lived in God's service, and pray that we may all be united in the communion of saints. We pray for those who have died, "because we still hold them in our love, and because we trust that in God's presence those who have chosen to serve him will grow in his love, until they see him as he is" (BCP, p. 862).

Easter hymns are highly suitable, and the color white reflects the Resurrection spirit of the Burial Office. Expenses for the coffin and tombstone should be kept to a minimum. Flowers should be provided by the Church or family, and others should be urged to give money for some useful charitable or religious purpose as a memorial. A pall always covers the casket in Church to signify the equality of all before God. The coffin is to be closed prior to the service and remain so thereafter (BCP, p. 468), for our purpose is to commit, with due respect, the mortal remains (but not the person), to the grave and dust whence they came. Cremation is also permissible and sometimes desirable, but it should be used together with the service of Committal and the Burial Office, and the ashes should be disposed of reverently. For Christians, the death of loved ones, with all its sense of loss in this life, may be the beginning of a deeper sense of communion and spiritual growth, and a time to thank God "who gives us the victory through our Lord Jesus Christ" (1 Cor. 15:57).

Questions to Think About—VIII

a. Why should we tell others about Christianity? Isn't what they believe their own business?

b. If I try to do the will of God daily, why do I have to go to Church?

c. Does vocation mean that there is only one specific kind of work to which we are called?

d. If two people really love each other, isn't that the same thing as being married, and isn't what they do their own business, as long as they don't hurt each other or anyone else?

IX The Episcopal Church

269. **Q.** What is the Episcopal Church?

     A. The Episcopal Church is a part of Christ's One, Holy, Catholic, and Apostolic Church. It is an independent Christian body self-governing under God, with its own constitution and elected leadership. While independent, the Episcopal Church seeks to be loyal and obedient to the guidance of the Holy Spirit in the universal Church, and adheres firmly to the tradition and fellowship of its sister Churches in The Anglican Communion.

270. **Q.** What is the Anglican Communion?

     A. The Anglican Communion is an association of independent Churches which hold certain principles and traditions in common. Historically, all of these Churches are connected with the Church of England, and look to the Archbishop of Canterbury as a spiritual leader, "first among equals." The prayer books of the several Churches within the Anglican Communion, though they show considerable variety, witness to an essential unity in worship, doctrine, and order which reflects the tradition of the Catholic Church as it developed in England at the time of the Reformation and has been adapted to other national circumstances. The Anglican Communion does not claim to be the only true Church, but a part of it. It gladly recognizes that God works mightily in other communions and traditions of the Church as well, and strives to unite with them in fellowship and faith.

271. **Q.** Who is the founder of the Episcopal Church?

     A. The founder of the Church is Jesus Christ. Although various human agents and historical circumstances have influenced the customs and traditions of the Episcopal Church and other Anglican Churches, there has been a continuous, uninterrupted development, without fundamental change of faith or order since the time of the Apostles, who were ordained by Christ himself.

272. **Q.** Into what two great classes are Christians now divided?
A. Unfortunately the One Church of Christ is divided in many ways. The many divided churches are usually classed in two groups, generally called "Catholic" and "Protestant", though those are not entirely satisfactory terms. The "Catholic" Churches have endeavored to maintain their continuity with the ancient apostolic Church in their order of ministry, faith, and sacraments. Among these Churches are the Roman Catholic Church, including all those under the Bishop of Rome (called the Pope); the Orthodox Churches, whose tradition is mainly Greek and Eastern European, but also includes Asian and African elements; the Anglican Churches; and various other small bodies, some of them ancient, and some of which have broken away from Rome since the eighteenth century. The "Protestant" Churches are those which, beginning at the time of the Reformation in the sixteenth century, have made various changes in an attempt to reform the Church and bring it back to the purity of what they conceive the essence of Biblical religion to be. Unfortunately there is not unanimity as to what the exact faith and order of the New Testament Church had been, and so a wide diversity and, in some respects, historical discontinuity has resulted.

273. **Q.** On what basis does the Pope claim to be the spiritual ruler of all Christians?
A. The Pope claims to be the successor of Peter who, it is said, was the first Bishop of Rome. The Roman Catholic Church interprets the words of Christ in Matthew 16:18, "You are Peter, and on this rock I will build my church," as meaning that Christ appointed Peter (and his successors) to be the supreme head of the Church.

Q. How does the Anglican Communion respond to these claims that the Pope is the head of all Christians?

A. First, there is no clear evidence that Peter was ever acknowledged to be the Bishop of Rome in his own day or that he ever went there at all. The New Testament, including Acts 28 which tells of Paul's going to Rome, the letter of Paul to the Romans, and the letters of Paul written in Rome make no mention of Peter's work there. The "historical" evidence supporting Peter's work in Rome is much later and of uncertain value. Second, the words of Christ in Matthew 16:17-19 do not mean that he appointed Peter to be the head of the Church, for otherwise the disciples would not have come to Jesus to ask him which of them was to be the greatest (Mt. 18:1; Mk. 9:33-37). The "rock" (Greek *petra*) on which Jesus said he would build his Church was the confession of *faith* that Jesus was "the Christ, the Son of the living God," not the *person*, Peter (Greek *Petros*). The authority "to bind and loose" (Mt. 16:19), furthermore is given to all the disciples in Matthew 18:18 and John 20:23. In the first chapters of Acts, Peter does seem to be the leader of the disciples, but in Acts 15, Galatians 2, and elsewhere, he clearly seems to be subordinate to James, the brother of Jesus.

275. **Q.** Was the Church ever united under the Bishop of Rome?

A. No. The New Testament gives no indication that there was any Bishop of Rome at that time nor that Rome had the dominant position in the Church. Writing late in the first century, Clement calls himself "an elder," not "the bishop," and although he seems to have been a leader in the Roman Church, he makes no claims to universal authority. There were several patriarchates in the early Church, but none of them was universally recognized as being supreme.

276. **Q.** How did the Eastern and Western Churches become separated?

A. When the Roman Empire split in the late fourth century and the major capital became Constantinople, the Eastern Church, which was Greek in culture and language, developed independently of the Western Church, centered in Rome, which was mainly Latin in language and culture. In 867 these two branches of the one Catholic Church began to separate after numerous controversies of a theological and political nature. Although they occasionally came together after that, there was a complete break in 1054, after which there was virtually no communication between them until recent times.

277. **Q.** What were some of the chief causes of the Reformation in the Western Church?

A. Although Christianity spread throughout Europe and much of Asia and Africa during the centuries after the birth of our Lord, and although the Church survived persecution, barbarian conquests, and the rise of Islam, stagnation and corruption also infected the Church. Of course there were great Christians like Anselm, Francis of Assisi, and Thomas Aquinas, and monastic movements often tried to purify the Church, but their efforts were not sufficient. The Bible was not read by the people (most of whom could not read), and it was taught that the ordinary believer could not have direct access to God except through the hierarchy of the Church. There were many superstitions, and counterfeit relics with supposedly magical powers deceived the simple. The moral life of the clergy, including cardinals, bishops, and sometimes Popes, was often scandalous. From 1305 to 1378 the Popes abandoned Rome for Avignon in southern France, and from 1378 to 1417 there were two or even three, rival Popes. Bishoprics and even the Papacy were sold, or given as political favors, to completely unworthy recipients, including children. The Pope who excommunicated Luther, Leo X (1513-21), was made a Cardinal at the age of 14, and was crowned Pope four days after his ordination as priest and two days after his consecration as bishop, all because he was from the powerful and wealthy family of Medici. The Church of Rome also drew heavily on the financial resources of other countries to support the luxurious lives of the hierarchy and the lavish church buildings in Rome. All these things, together with the new questioning spirit of the Renaissance, the recovery of Greek learning and the knowledge of the Greek New Testament, led many people to be dissatisfied with the debased Church which they saw.

278. **Q.** Who were the first reformers, and what were the results of their work?

A. There were, of course, many reformers and reform movements within the Church, but the incident which is generally considered to be the start of the historical movement called the Reformation was Martin Luther's posting of his Ninety-Five Theses on the door of the castle church in Wittenberg, Germany, in 1517. It began as an attack on the debased practice of indulgences, but when the authorities rejected his call for reform, Luther expanded his attack. His reform movement quickly spread to other areas in Germany and led to the beginning of the Lutheran Church. Luther's watch-cry was "justification by faith." In Switzerland, Ulrich Zwingli also led a reform movement in Zurich, and later John Calvin an even more influential one in Geneva which inspired the Reformed and Presbyterian Churches. Elsewhere Anabaptists were making more radical reforms which virtually denied the traditional concept of the Church and led to individualistic faith and congregational polity. All these movements emphasized the authority of the Bible as the standard of faith, and repudiated the Pope and the Roman Church wherever they departed from scripture. They founded new churches, mostly without bishops, and with substantial changes in teaching concerning the sacraments and ministry. This represented a marked discontinuity with the historic Catholic Churches of both the East and the West. These Protestant Churches have continued to this day, many of them growing greatly in numbers, and have contributed much to the world and the whole Church.

279. **Q.** When was the Christian Church established in England?

A. We do not know who first brought the gospel to England, but it was probably travellers from France or soldiers in the first two centuries. We know that in 314 three bishops from England attended a Church council in Arles, in southern France, so the Church must have been widely spread in England by that time. In 596 Pope Gregory I sent a mission of about forty monks, headed by Augustine, to begin work in England. They landed in Kent, were able to plant the Church, and Augustine was later made the first Archbishop of Canterbury, where their work was centered.

280. **Q.** Why was it necessary to send this mission if the Church was already there?

A. After the Roman Empire withdrew its troops from England in 407, the British Isles were invaded repeatedly by pagan Angles, Saxons, and Jutes, who destroyed churches, massacred some of the inhabitants, and drove the rest to the west: Cornwall, Wales, and Ireland. From Ireland, where the Church had been organized by Patrick about 430 AD, a mission was sent to Scotland and northern England, headed by Columba, in 563. Thus the Church in the British Isles already existed in the north and the west, although it had been destroyed in the south and the east, and was isolated from Rome. Later these two Churches united and became part of the Western Church under Rome. Gradually the whole of the British Isles was brought into the Church, and from England missionaries evangelized much of northern Europe.

281. **Q.** What was the situation in England at the beginning of the Reformation?

A. The Church flourished in England, but there was increasing restiveness because of corruptions in the Church and the domination of Rome. The reform movement of John Wycliffe in the fourteenth century, although suppressed, was not forgotten. The English, like other European peoples resented the interference of the Pope in their internal political affairs and the large amount of money which Rome claimed.

282. **Q.** When did the Church of England declare its independence from Rome?

A. The Church of England became independent in 1534 when Parliament passed the Act of Supremacy, which stated that the monarch was titular head of the Church, and not the Pope. There was no real reformation at this time, however. The Mass continued to be said in Latin, and non-scriptural doctrines and practices were left largely untouched. Nevertheless, a new translation of the Bible into English was authorized in 1536, and this was widely read, along with the writings of the reformers, when they could be obtained.

283. **Q.** Is it correct to say that Henry VIII was founder of the Church of England?

A. No, for the Church of England remained the same in all essentials as it was before, and therefore no new Church was founded. The same Church which had been the Catholic Church in England continued without interruption or discontinuity. The Church of England did not separate itself from Rome, although it declared its independence from the Pope. This had previously been done by the kings of France, without thereby leaving the Church. The occasion of Henry's dispute with the Pope was his desire for an annulment of his marriage to Catherine of Aragon, who had previously married his elder brother. The Popes had often granted annulments to kings and nobles in similar cases, but for political reasons Henry was refused. At Henry's death in 1547, the same bishops and clergy still led the Church, with the same sacraments and creeds, and virtually the same Latin liturgy. It would not be correct to say, therefore, that Henry founded a new church, nor even that he reformed an old one. It was the same Church, and there were no thorough reforms until after his death.

284. **Q.** When did the Church of England carry out more thorough reforms?
A. The Church of England carried out thorough reforms for the first time under Edward VI, between 1547 and 1553.

285. **Q.** Was the Reformation in England similar to the Reformation in other countries in Europe?
A. No. Most of the Protestant Churches in Europe separated themselves not only from the Pope, but also from many aspects of the Catholic tradition of the Church, especially in the sacraments and the apostolic ministry and liturgy. The Church of England was careful to keep what it considered to be all the essentials of the Catholic tradition, including bishops ordained in the apostolic succession, as well as the ministry of priests and deacons, the sacraments instituted by Christ, the historic creeds, and the essential liturgy, translated into English and purged of its unscriptural corruptions. The Church of England may therefore be said to have maintained its catholicity unimpaired and strengthened by a more Biblical emphasis in its doctrine and practice.

286. **Q.** What reforms were made in the Church of England?
A. During the reign of Henry VIII, the Bible was made available in English in all the churches, and some of the abuses of the practice of veneration of images and relics were eliminated. Under the new king, Edward VI, reform

measures increased. In 1549 Thomas Cranmer, Archbishop of Canterbury, together with other Church leaders, issued the first *Book of Common Prayer* in the name of the king. It contained a liturgy in English, retaining the heart of the ancient liturgies, but purged of the later medieval accretions, so that it was both catholic and reformed. The emphasis on the Bible in the Church services, and the scriptural basis of doctrines in the Articles of Religion made the Church of England evangelical in its teaching and practice. Communion in both kinds became the rule, the clergy were no longer required to be celibate, indulgences were forbidden, and many other reforms took place.

287. **Q.** Did the Church of England proceed smoothly with its reforms after that?
A. No. During the later part of Edward's reign, this boy king was surrounded by unscrupulous advisors who for political reasons used the radical reformist cause to carry the Protestant principle so far that the Church was in danger of losing its catholic heritage. When Edward died at the age of sixteen in 1553, he was succeeded by his half-sister Mary, who was a strong supporter of Rome and of her mother's country, Spain. She quickly brought the Church back under Rome, suppressed the prayer book, returned the service to Latin, and restored many of the practices which had recently been eliminated.

288. **Q.** What changes came about with the accession of Queen Elizabeth I?
A. After Mary died, and Elizabeth became queen in 1558, many of the reforms that had been made under Edward VI were restored, the prayer book reissued in a revised form, and the doctrine of the Church of England was defined in the Thirty-Nine Articles of Religion (BCP, pp. 867-876).

289. **Q.** When was the final break with Rome?
A. Not until 1570 did Pope Pius V excommunicate Elizabeth and declare the Church of England in heresy. For twelve years, therefore, although the Church of England had resumed the reforms made during the reign of Edward VI, it remained in communion with Rome, and Rome made no statements concerning the validity of its ministry, sacraments, and doctrine. If the Church was indeed in heresy and its sacraments invalid, the Pope should have warned the English people twelve years earlier that they were endangering their salvation. The fact that he did not do so makes it seem that the 1570 decision was based on political reasons.

290. **Q.** What was the character of the Church of England from the time of Queen Elizabeth I?
A. The Church of England was Catholic in its orders of ministry within the apostolic succession, its two major sacraments of Baptism and the Eucharist, its liturgy inherited from ancient times, and its acceptance of the historic creeds of the undivided Church. At the same time it accepted and made its own many of the fresh insights of the Protestant Reformation and redefined its doctrine to make sure it was in strict accord with the Scripture. It also incorporated some of the features of the Eastern Orthodox liturgy into its own. In this way it sought to maintain continuity with the past and also to accept what was good from other traditions. During the long struggle to reform the Church, mistakes were unfortunately made at various times and injustice done on both sides, and often political rather than theological factors were decisive for both Protestants and Catholics. In spite of this, it can be said that the emerging Church of England was both catholic and reformed, with an emphasis on the gospel that was truly evangelical. It was also a national Church, independent and self-governing. The Church of England did not try to impose

its structure on other nations outside the British Isles but respected the right of each nation to form its own national Church.

291. **Q.** Did this Anglican form of the Church spread to other countries?

A. Yes. Through the missionary work of the Church of England, Anglicanism spread to many other countries, at first mainly to British colonies, but then to many other countries throughout the world. Under different circumstances in Scotland, where the established Church was Presbyterian, the Episcopal Church of Scotland became an independent national Church which maintained its Catholic and Anglican heritage.

292. **Q.** When did Anglicanism first come to North America?

A. Although there were isolated cases of Anglican worship in the New World when English explorers or would-be colonists came there in the sixteenth century, the first permanent planting of the Church was at Jamestown, Virginia, in 1607. There the Chaplain, Robert Hunt, led Morning and Evening Prayer every day, and on June 20, 1607, celebrated the Holy Eucharist for the first time. In other colonies, too, Anglican churches were started, and although there was opposition in many areas where Anglicans were in the minority, the numbers grew. There were no bishops, however, and there was little communication between the colonies, so no organization bound them together.

293. **Q.** What happened to these Anglican churches at the time of the Revolution?

A. The American Revolution caused a serious crisis in the life of the Church. It was officially the Church of *England*, and the clergy who had *all* been ordained in England and had taken an oath of allegiance to the king, were placed in a very difficult position. Many of them felt it their duty to remain loyal to the king and obedient to the Bishop of London, and many of the clergy and laity fled to Canada. Even though many of the leaders of the Revolution, from Washington on down, were Anglicans, the Church was looked on with suspicion because of the English connection, and some of the clergy and laity were persecuted and Church property destroyed. All financial support from England ceased, and in areas where the Church had been established, its lands and sometimes buildings were taken away. Cut off from the Mother Church, without bishops or other widely recognized leaders, with no organization or written constitution, the separated and scattered churches were weakened and demoralized.

294. **Q.** How did the separated churches in the various states succeed in forming a national Church?
A. Attempts were made in the various states to achieve some kind of organization, but it was William White, rector of Christ Church, Philadelphia, and chaplain of the Continental Congress, who in 1782 first put forward a plan for an Episcopal Church with a federal organization and lay as well as clerical representation in its governing body, a distinctive, new idea in church governance at that time. It was White who presided at most of the meetings which led up to the formation of the Church, and guided it to form its Constitution and Canons. White's plan, however, would not have created the Episcopal Church as we know it, for bishops were still lacking.

295. **Q.** How were bishops secured for the new Church in the United States of America?
A. In 1783, The Reverend Dr. Samuel Seabury was elected by the clergy of Connecticut to be their bishop and was asked to go to England to seek consecration. The English bishops were unable to consecrate him, however, without a special Act of Parliament, for he could not swear loyalty to the king and serve in Connecticut. He therefore went

113

to the independent Episcopal Church of Scotland, where he was consecrated by three of the Scottish bishops in Aberdeen on November 14, 1784, and became the first Anglican bishop consecrated to serve outside the British Isles. He returned to Connecticut the following year and ordained four candidates to the diaconate, the first Anglican ordinations in North America. Meanwhile in England, an act was passed to enable Archbishops of Canterbury and York to consecrate bishops to serve in other countries, and in 1787 William White was consecrated as Bishop of Pennsylvania, and Samuel Provoost as Bishop of New York. In 1790 James Madison was consecrated, also in London, as Bishop of Virginia. In 1792 the four American bishops consecrated Thomas Claggett as Bishop of Maryland, and the new Church was no longer dependent on others for ordinations.

296. **Q.** How did the Episcopal Church achieve its unity and organization?

A. After preliminary meetings in 1785 and 1786 the General Convention of 1789, meeting in Philadelphia, set the pattern for the Protestant Episcopal Church in the United States of America and achieved its national unity. This decisive convention adopted a Constitution and Canons, and *The Book of Common Prayer,* which maintained the essentials of the Catholic and Anglican heritage, with distinctly American adaptations (BCP, pp. 8-11). Not only was this of great importance to the Episcopal Church in the United States, but it also showed that Anglicanism could adapt itself to different situations, and this was the first of many independent national Anglican Churches outside the British Isles.

297. **Q.** What are the main features of the organization of the Episcopal Church?

A. The Episcopal Church is a confederation of dioceses which, as its name implies, are led by bishops, who are the chief pastors in their respective dioceses, and who, with the clergy under them, are entrusted with the spiritual guidance of the people. But just as the President of the United States, or the governors in the states, cannot act except in accordance with the law of the land, so the bishops, clergy, and laity of the Episcopal Church must always act in conformity with the Constitution and Canons of the Episcopal Church, the prayer book, and the decisions of the national legislative body, the General Covention. Far from being a Church ruled by an autocratic hierarchy, the Episcopal Church is one of the most democratic institutions in the world, in which, at all levels, the laity and clergy have an equal voice and responsibility. This is not because we distrust our bishops, but because we believe that the Holy Spirit leads the whole Church, and that every sincere and faithful Christian can hear the voice of God, is called to be an apostle for Christ, and to share in the priesthood of all believers (1 Pet. 2:9). The bishops of the various dioceses are all elected by the laity and clergy, and rectors are called to parishes by duly elected vestries. The General Convention meets every three years and is the highest legislative body of the Church. It consists of two houses, the House of Bishops, and the House of Deputies, which is made up of four clerical and four lay deputies from each diocese, elected at annual diocesan conventions. Only the General Convention has the authority to change the Constitution and Canons of the Church or to revise the prayer book and Hymnal. It decides on a budget and draws up a program for the Church at home and abroad. For the carrying out of the program there is an Executive Council, and its various departments assist the dioceses in carrying out the Church's work. The Presiding Bishop (or Primate), who is elected by the House of Bishops and approved by the House of Deputies, presides over the Executive Council and the House of Bishops, and is the chief executive officer and spiritual head of the Church.

298. **Q.** How has the Episcopal Church endeavored to obey Christ's command to be his witnesses "to the end of the earth" (Acts 1:8)?

A. From the first the Church has had to be a missionary Church, building where there had been no Church before. In 1821 The Domestic and Foreign Missionary Society of the Episcopal Church was formed, and in 1835 it was declared that all members of the Church were automatically members of the Society. This is as it should be, for to be a Christian implies living and witnessing to Christ, and a "church" which is not missionary is not the Church of Christ. The Church grew from small beginnings on the East Coast to be a national Church in all the States, and the Episcopal Church has sent missionaries to foreign lands to establish the Church throughout the world. In this we work with other Churches, especially in the Anglican Communion, to build independent, self-governing national Churches in each country or region. All members of the Episcopal Church have the privilege and responsibility of supporting this work. In addition our Church has many programs in our own country to meet the spiritual, economic, and social needs of individuals and groups, and all of us can share in supporting this work.

299. **Q.** In what way are the independent Anglican Churches kept together?

A. The Anglican Communion, as it is called, is a free association. There is no compulsion, yet all are united in spirit. The Churches of the Anglican Communion share the same doctrines, and our various liturgies in the prayer books of each Church derive from the same common tradition. All Anglicans are united in giving to the Archbishop of Canterbury spiritual precedence within the Communion, although this does not imply any authority in other provinces. About every ten years there is a Conference at Lambeth Palace in London, the official residence of the Archbishop of Canterbury. To this are invited Anglican bishops from all over the world, and common tasks and problems are discussed and resolutions passed. An Anglican Consultative Council, made up of clergy and laity, carries on work as required for the various national Churches or Provinces on a continuing basis. There have been Anglican Congresses and various programs of cooperation to coordinate the mission and work of the Anglican Churches throughout the world. Although none of these has any legislative authority binding on the various Churches, their influence is important in cementing the ties of unity, and in giving guidance on moral, social, evangelistic, and ecumenical challenges which face the Church. Increasingly there is a sense of our mutual responsibility and interdependence, and the need for cooperation and unity to meet the great tasks before us.

300. **Q.** Do the Episcopal Church and the Anglican Communion seek unity with other Christian Churches?
A. Yes. We believe that it is the will of God that we should all be One in Christ, as Christ himself prayed (Jn. 17:21). We are therefore working to break down the barriers that separate us from each other. In the World Council of Churches and the National Council of Churches we have found many areas where we can come closer together with others and work for common goals. There have also been discussions on the possibility of full, organic, union with various churches to form a united Church which is fully catholic, fully reformed, and fully evangelical. For Anglicans there are four essential principles which are prerequisites for organic union. These are known as the Chicago-Lambeth Quadrilateral (BCP, pp. 876-78), first adopted by the House of Bishops in Chicago in 1886, and made a resolution of the Lambeth Conference in 1888. These four principles state that: (1) the Old and New Testaments contain all that is necessary for salvation and are the rule and ultimate standard of faith; (2) the Apostles'

Creed and the Nicene Creed are sufficient statements of faith; (3) the two sacraments of Baptism and the Eucharist were ordained by Christ for the Church; and (4) the historic episcopate is necessary for the people called by God into the unity of the Church.

While recognizing God's work in other traditions, and being conscious of the many shortcomings of our own witness in the world, we believe that the Episcopal Church and the Anglican Communion with their treasures of old traditions and new discoveries have a unique contribution to the worldwide Church of Christ. We look forward to the day when we can bring our treasures with us into the unity of the true witnessing fellowship of Christ's servants, the One Holy Catholic and Apostolic Church.

Questions to Think About—IX

a. Is it really necessary to have a national, organizational, institutional Church?
b. Is it necessary for a Church to have a detailed definition of the faith, and to exclude those who do not agree with it?
c. Why do we need ordained ministers? Why is the historic episcopate important?
d. Wouldn't a big united Church be too bureaucratic, and isn't there an advantage in having smaller, diverse Churches with friendly competition?

An Outline of the Life of Christ

(The order of events is partially uncertain)

Annunciation to Mary, Visitation	Luke 1:26–56
Annunciation to Joseph	Matt. 1:18–25
Birth, adoration of the shepherds	Luke 2:1–20
Birth, manifestation to the wise men	Matt. 2:1–12
Circumcision and presentation in the temple. Return to Nazareth	Luke 2:21–39
Visit to Jerusalem at age of twelve	Luke 2:40–52
Jesus baptized by John	Mark 1:9–11
Temptation in the wilderness	Luke 4:1–13
The call of the four in Galilee	Mark 1:16–20
Marriage feast in Cana of Galilee	John 2:1–11
Jesus teaches and heals in Capernaum	Mark 1:21–34
Itinerant preaching in Galilee	Mark 1:35–45
Nicodemus sees Jesus in Jerusalem	John 3:1–21
Return to Galilee by Samaria; the Water of Life	John 4:1–42
Conflicts with the scribes and Pharisees	Mark 2:1–3:5
Pharisees plot with Herodians to destory Jesus	Mark 3:6
Jesus chooses twelve apostles	Mark 3:13–19
The Sermon on the Mount	Matt. 5–7
Jesus teaches the people in parables	Mark 4:1–34
Crossing the lake and stilling the storm	Mark 4:35–41
Gerasense demoniac and Jairus' daughter	Mark 5
Rejection at Nazareth	Mark 6:1–6, Luke 4:16–30
The mission and return of the Twelve	Mark 6:7–32
Feeding of the five thousand (the Jews?)	Mark 6:31–46
Jesus goes through the region of Tyre	Mark 7:24–30
Return to Galilee and the Decapolis	Mark 7:31
Feeding of the four thousand (Gentiles?)	Mark 8:1–10
Confession of Peter: Caesarea Philippi	Mark 8:27–30

Jesus foretells his death	Mark 8:31–38
The transfiguration	Mark 9:2–13
To Jerusalem, walking east of Jordan	Mark 10:1
Mission of the Seventy	Luke 10:1–24
Teaching on the way to Jerusalem	Luke 10:25–18:34
Bartimaeus and Zachaeus in Jericho	Luke 18:35–19:10
Raising of Lazarus in Bethany	John 11:1–54
The entry into Jerusalem	Mark 11:1–11
Jesus cleanses the temple	Mark 11:15–19
Conflicts with religious leaders	Mark 11:27–12:44
Final teachings and predictions	Matthew 24–25
The Last Supper	Mark 14:12–25
Jesus washes the disciples' feet	John 13:1–17
The last discourses	John 14–16
The high-priestly prayer	John 17
Agony in Gethsemane, betrayal and arrest	Mark 14:26–52
Trial before the high-priest	Mark 14:53–65
The denial of Peter	Mark 14:66–72
Trial before Pilate	Mark 15:1–15
Scourging and crucifixion	Mark 15:15–41
Burial in Joseph of Arimathea's tomb	Mark 15:42–47
Resurrection	Matt. 28,
	Luke 24,
	Mark 16,
	John 20–21
Ascension	Luke 24:51,
	Acts 1:1–11

Church History Chart

with special reference to Anglicanism

30 AD   Pentecost, beginning of apostolic church in Jerusalem; Peter and John; seven deacons ordained

30-45   Stephen martyred; Christians take gospel to the world; conversion of Paul; gentile Christians

45-60   Council of Jerusalem; Paul's missionary journeys; planting of the church in many lands

64   Persecution of Christians under Nero in Rome; probable martyrdoms of Peter and Paul

70   Destruction of Jerusalem; persecutions, but continued growth of church and Christian writings

90-310   Development of organization and doctrine; Ignatius 110; Justin 150; Irenaeus 202; Clement of Alexandria 210; Tertullian 230; Origen 251; Cyprian 258

311   Edict of Toleration under Constantine; Christianity becomes official religion of empire

325   Council of Nicea; Constantinople 381; Ephesus 431; Chalcedon 451; credal statements; Athanasius

410   Rome sacked; Ambrose 397; Jerome 420; Augustine of Hippo 430; Benedict of Nursia 543; monasticism

563   Columba's mission to Iona; Gregory sends Augustine (of Canterbury) to Kent 596

664   Synod of Whitby; Theodore of Tarsus 690; Bede 735; Willibrord 739; Boniface 754

800   Charlemagne revives Roman Empire in the West; Moslems defeated at Tours 732

1054   East-West split; Norman conquest 1066; Crusades 1095-1291; Anselm 1109; Waldo 1176; Francis 1226; Thomas Aquinas 1274

1384   Wyclif translates Bible and advocates reforms; Hus of Bohemia martyred at Constance 1415

1517   Luther's 95 Theses; Zwingli in Zurich 1519; Anabaptists 1524; Calvin in Geneva 1536

1534	Act of Supremacy: English Church declares independence from Rome but few reforms under Henry VIII; Great Bible 1539
1545-63	Council of Trent; Loyola's Jesuit Order recognized in 1540, works to counter Protestant expansion; Francis Xavier
1549	Book of Common Prayer and major reforms under Edward VI and Cranmer; second prayer book 1552
1553	Mary Tudor returns church to Rome; persecutions; Latimer, Ridley, Cranmer and others burned 1555-6
1558	Elizabeth reinstitutes reforms; excommunicated by Pope 1570; 39 Articles 1571; Puritan controversies
1607	Jamestown (Church of England); Plymouth Pilgrims (Separatist) 1620; Massachusetts Bay (Puritans) 1629
1636	Roger Williams in Rhode Island, Baptists 1639; Maryland, Roman Catholics 1632; Quakers 1656
1649	England Commonwealth; Restoration 1660; 1662 prayer book; SPCK 1699 and SPG 1701 help colonial church.
1734	First Great Awakening; Wesley starts Methodist societies 1739; deism and formalism attacked
1775	American Revolution; White proposes Episcopal Church 1782; Seabury consecrated 1784
1789	Convention in Philadelphia adopts prayer book, Constitution and Canons of Episcopal Church in USA
1833	Oxford Movement; first Lambeth Conference 1867; World Missionary Conference 1910; 1928 prayer book
1948	World Council of Churches; Third Anglican Congress, Toronto 1963; first meeting of Anglican Consultative Council 1971

Chronology of the Bible

Pre-History	Creation and Fall, *Genesis 1—3*; The Flood, the Tower of Babel, *Genesis 6—11*
2000-1600 BC	Age of the Patriarchs: Abraham, Isaac, Jacob; Joseph, *Genesis 11—50*
1280	Moses, Exodus from Egypt, Ten Commandments, *Exodus-Deuteronomy*
1240	Joshua leads Israel into Promised Land of Canaan, *Joshua*
1200-1050	Age of the Judges (Deborah, Gideon, Jephthah, Samson), *Judges, Ruth*
1050-1000	Samuel, the beginning of the Monarchy, Saul and David, *1 Samuel*
1000-970	David consolidates the Kingdom of Israel, *2 Samuel*
970-940	Solomon builds the first Temple in Jerusalem, *1 Kings 1—11*
930	Division of the kingdom; Israel-north, Judah-south, *1 Kings 12*
860	Elijah the prophet resists King Ahab, *1 Kings 17—22*
850	Elisha the prophet follows Elijah, *2 Kings 1—13*
721	Israel (northern kingdom) destroyed by Assyria, people exiled, *2 Kings 17, Amos, Hosea*
701	Jerusalem besieged by Assyria, Judah devastated, *2 Kings 18—19, Isaiah*
621	Josiah's reform; Babylon conquers Assyria in 612, *2 Kings 22—23, Jeremiah*
587	Judah falls to Babylon; *Jeremiah*. Captivity: *Ezekiel*. Cyrus of Persia conquers Babylon, 539, *2 Kings 24—25, Ezekiel*
538	Persian Empire allows some Jews to return from exile, *Ezra 1—6, Haggai, Zechariah*
444	Nehemiah builds up Jerusalem; Ezra returns in 428, *Ezra, Nehemiah*
332	Greek conquest under Alexander. Palestine under Ptolemies 301, and Seleucids 198

167	Revolt and victory of Maccabees, *Apocrypha*
63	Roman conquest of Palestine. Herod the Great 37-4
4 BC?	Birth of Christ; Birth of John the Baptist, *Matthew, Luke*
30 AD?	Crucifixion, Resurrection, Ascension, *Four Gospels*. Pentecost and the growth of the Apostolic Church, *Acts, Letters*
47	Paul's first missionary journey, *Acts 13-14*
49	Council of Jerusalem, *Acts 15*
50-60	Paul's last three journeys, *Acts 15—28*
64	Persecution under Nero. Death of Peter and Paul?
70	Destruction of Jerusalem and the Temple. Spread of Christianity under persecution.

(Note: Some of the above dates are uncertain. They refer to the events recorded, not to the dates in which the books were written.)

Comments, Suggestions, Criticisms

If there are additional subjects you think should be included in this book, or any which should be treated more fully,

If you have other changes to suggest,

If you have found errors,

If you would like to tell us what parts were most or least helpful,

If you have questions,

you are invited to write:

The Editor
Forward Movement Publications
412 Sycamore Street
Cincinnati, Ohio 45202

For further study: Forward Movement publishes many books and pamphlets on the subjects introduced in *Questions on the Way*. All are listed in the FM catalog.

Born in Shanghai, China, the son of a medical missionary, *Beverley D. Tucker* has served his entire ministry as a priest in the Episcopal Church in Japan. He has worked in parish settings there, one of which is described in his book *God Gave the Increase,* and on seminary and university faculties. He is now on the faculty of the English department of Doshisha University in Kyoto, while also working in St. Agnes Church and Bishop Williams Seminary.

William H. Swatos, Jr. has served as a priest in the domestic mission field, currently in the Diocese of Quincy (Illinois). He is also a sociologist of religion and has held a number of college and university appointments. His books include *Into Denominationalism: The Anglican Metamorphosis* and *Religious Sociology: Interfaces and Boundaries.*